UNBOUND

Ukrainian Canadians Writing Home

Unbound

Ukrainian Canadians Writing Home

EDITED BY
LISA GREKUL AND LINDY LEDOHOWSKI

UNIVERSITY OF TORONTO PRESS
Toronto Buffalo London

© University of Toronto Press 2016
Toronto Buffalo London
www.utppublishing.com
Printed in the U.S.A.

Reprinted 2018

ISBN 978-1-4426-3109-0

∞ Printed on acid-free, 100% post-consumer recycled paper.

Library and Archives Canada Cataloguing in Publication

Unbound : Ukrainian Canadians writing home / edited by
Lisa Grekul and Lindy Ledohowski.

Includes bibliographical references.
ISBN 978-1-4426-3109-0 (bound)

1. Canadian literature (English) – Ukrainian Canadian authors.   2. Canadian literature (English) – Ukrainian Canadian authors – Bibliography.   3. Ukrainians – Canada – History.   I. Grekul, Lisa, 1972–, editor   II. Ledohowski, Lindy, 1976–, editor

PS8235.U4U53 2016   C810.8'0891791   C2015-906500-3

This publication was made possible by the financial support of the Ukrainian Canadian Foundation of Taras Shevchenko.

University of Toronto Press acknowledges the financial assistance to its publishing program of the Canada Council for the Arts and the Ontario Arts Council, an agency of the government of Ontario.

Contents

Foreword: "Write Your Stories Down; Make Your Voices Heard"   vii
WERONIKA SUCHACKA

Acknowledgments   xiii

Introduction: Ukrainian Canadian Poet Pedagogues   3
LINDY LEDOHOWSKI

1 Language Lessons   23
JANICE KULYK KEEFER

2 Eight Things   41
ELIZABETH BACHINSKY

3 Am I Ukrainian?   65
MARSHA FORCHUK SKRYPUCH

4 Bringing Back Memory   73
MARUSYA BOCIURKIW

5 Tuteshni   86
ERÍN MOURE

6 Putting the *Baba* Back in the Book   100
DARIA SALAMON

7 The Gulag, the Crypt and the Gallows: Sites of Ukrainian Canadian Desire   109
MYRNA KOSTASH

Conclusion: Ukrainian Identities On(the)Line: Writing Ethnicity in a Time of Crisis   121
LISA GREKUL

Appendix: Bibliography of English-Language Ukrainian Canadian Literature   137

References   141

Contributors   149

Foreword: "Write Your Stories Down; Make Your Voices Heard"[1]

WERONIKA SUCHACKA

It's 2006; I am sitting in a Ukrainian Canadian literature classroom. Let me be clear: I am not Canadian; I am not Ukrainian; I am not Ukrainian Canadian for that matter, and I do not live in Canada. I am a Polish girl studying at a German university, but I listen avidly, even impatiently, to a Ukrainian Canadian voice, the first I have ever heard. It is beautiful and powerful in its message. With other Polish and German students, I listen to a visiting professor, Janice Kulyk Keefer. I am entranced not only by the content of her talk: her sense of history, a sense that a part of official European history has been connected to the official history of North America by the personal histories and stories of Ukrainian immigrants and their offspring; or her sense of identity, a sense that these official and private accounts are expressive of complicated as well as complex experience and existence. I am also enchanted by the way the nature of Ukrainian-ness in Canada is revealed to me; I am enchanted by Kulyk Keefer's use of language, its poetic melody and the heightened sensitivity that each of her utterances displays. The writer becomes to me the embodiment of poetry and each class a journey into a completely unknown world, its past and present.

At the time, I also develop a deep fascination with Kulyk Keefer's writings. It is in her class that I read *The Green Library*, a novel that continues to impress me whenever I reread it. But thanks to the author, I also learn about other Ukrainian Canadian writers/artists and their works: Myrna Kostash's non-fiction, William Kurelek's paintings, and John Paskievich's documentary. It is also in this class that I hear such names as Marusya Bociurkiw, Mary Borsky, and Lisa Grekul for the first time. I virtually devour every piece of information I am provided with and I read every text assigned, but eager for more I spend hours in libraries and online in front of my computer, seeking more about Ukrainian Canadian literature. Later, when I do my MA and then PhD research, I experience how difficult it is to hunt down Ukrainian Canadian texts in Europe. Although German university libraries are wonderfully equipped, Ukrainian Canadian books are rarely available, and thus the only option left to me is ordering books from North America. The arrival of long-awaited books is a great experience on its own, and each book is treated by me as treasure. I am deeply grateful for my past scholarships and present fellowship, thanks to which I can afford those books. At that point, I would never have expected that discovering Ukrainian Canadian voices would take me to Canada, where I could literally hear those voices.

In 2009 I went to Toronto and Edmonton for my PhD research trip. I met Ukrainian Canadian writers and scholars in person, and each encounter became one of the most exhilarating moments of my life. Every scholar who is enthusiastic about the field she is working in will understand my excitement when I met with people whose work I so much admire. What was even more stimulating about these meetings was that each of them opened the door to my meetings with other Ukrainian Canadian writers. I was honoured with Janice Kulyk Keefer and her family's hospitality; I also had the pleasure of listening to her inspiring ideas about identity and literature and of being guided by her through questions about Ukrainian Canadian literature, which only multiplied for me. Thanks to her, I was able to meet a wonderful young scholar and writer, Lindy Ledohowski, whose work strongly influenced my PhD thesis after my return to Europe. I was inspired by our exchange of ideas but also by the information I received from her about authors like Elizabeth Bachinsky and Daria Salamon, whose works I was unfamiliar with at that time; I was about to explore them, having returned from Canada. It was through Ledohowski that I met Jars Balan in Edmonton. And it was only much later that I learned of the young adult fiction of Marsha Forchuk Skrypuch; I had been unfamiliar with her genre, but hers is a voice worth hearing.

The kindness I experienced from Kulyk Keefer and Ledohowski was also extended to me by Marusya Bociurkiw. I will never forget how warmly I was welcomed by her and how fascinating our conversation about the complexity of memory, history, and identity was, which to my great joy she later described on her blog. My final destination in Canada was Edmonton, where I went to meet Myrna Kostash, who, like Kulyk Keefer, has always been for me an icon of Ukrainian Canadian literature. I was hardly able to keep up with her as she showed me around Edmonton, taking me to different cultural, literary, and artistic events, which I probably would never have experienced had it not been for her. It was also thanks to her that I learned about the poetry of Erín Moure – another fascinating and crucial point in my discovery of Ukrainian Canadian literature.

I have started on a personal note here because, having studied Ukrainian Canadian literature, I have come to see it as highly contextual and deeply personal. At the same time, however, following Sonia Mycak, I see it as highly political in the sense that through it, Ukrainian Canadian writers have made Ukrainian Canadians visible and audible; as Mycak notes, "whilst these authors may not see themselves as being involved in any struggle ... the author has become the site of identity and a new point of centrality from which the previously peripheral Canadian-Ukrainian voice now speaks."[2] This sense of the author as a "site of identity" becomes evident particularly when we take into account that the most prominent contemporary Ukrainian Canadian writers are also scholars and teachers. For instance, Kostash has been and is a journalist and teacher, but she is probably best-known for being a pioneer in the genre of creative non-fiction. Kulyk Keefer has published poems, short stories, novels, and countless scholarly works and has spent her professional career as an English professor. Bociurkiw is a writer, professor, and film-maker, while Salamon is both a professional writer and a schoolteacher. Likewise, Bachinsky and Moure are poets and teachers. Skrypuch's books fill Canadian classrooms and are widely read by and taught to schoolchildren. The sampling of voices collected in this book gives a sense of the poets, novelists, non-fiction writers, playwrights, film-makers, lecturers, essayists, journalists, editors, and authors of scholarly studies who engage in many of these activities often and simultaneously. To use Mycak's words, "Put quite simply it is very difficult to classify ... [their] texts."[3]

In the spirit of these writers, who are not afraid to reinstate the speaking "I" of the text,[4] I will continue by telling you how I, a non-Canadian and non-Ukrainian, came to read, study, and love this body of literature. The brief description of my encounters with Ukrainian Canadian literature should signal that during my explorations of it I have become particularly drawn to Ukrainian Canadian women writers. As already stated here, these "sites of identity" are authors and critics as well as teachers and thus their writing is both creative and scholarly. But that is not the only reason why their works are so inspiring. I have long been mesmerized by their stories also because of the assured voices in which they are told and because of the deconstructive perspectives from which they are often presented. Their stories bend genres, and the words in them are not limited to the page or the classroom.[5] They invite readers to rethink, reinterpret, and even retell or rewrite them; the readers too become their subjects and authors.

In this respect, it is important to mention here Grekul's final message in the introduction to her 2005 study: "*Write your stories down; make your voices heard*,"[6] which vests equal responsibility for the future of Ukrainian Canadian literature in critics, scholars, writers, *and* readers.[7] She encourages readers to become writers recording their experiences; she wants to "inspire" them "to set down their stories."[8] Likewise, Kostash champions the cooperation of "writers [who] are also readers, ... and readers [who] often write."[9] As Mycak puts it, "the discursive nature of both authorship and the text"[10] in Ukrainian Canadian literature is clear. And while the importance of the author in this literature should be emphasized,[11] it is interesting that the writing project that many Ukrainian Canadian authors embark upon (one that, I suspect, shares features with many other minoritized writings) invites the reader to participate in a dialogue, one in which author, critic, and reader share and build knowledge. This body of literature does not evoke a scholarly hierarchy wherein the critic theorizes the authors' works and offers the reader important insights; rather, it sees scholars/writers asking questions of themselves and their readers as they engage in writings that concern various issues.[12] Quite simply, this book is about that close interaction between writers and readers, a relationship that many of these authors take very seriously.

One element in this two-way relationship enacted by Ukrainian Canadian literature relates to ethnicity. In many Ukrainian Canadian works, time (past and present) mingles with space (Ukraine and Canada), thereby forming the protagonists' identities.[13] This temporal and spatial commingling creates an interesting dynamic in which "the unfinished business of ethnic identity formation and articulation"[14] plays out. The works presented in this book offer excellent examples of this kind of play. These selections include speaking personae who are often stranded between multiple and seemingly mutually exclusive elements that construct identity. Their present is infused with the past, and each space – be it Canada or Ukraine – is infused with the other, absent one. The authors of these selections show us an identity that is often "caught in the spaces between longing and loss."[15]

While it is evident that "ethnic identity still matters"[16] for Ukrainian Canadians, interestingly, it also matters for a non–Ukrainian Canadian reader. Just like Ukrainian Canadian literature in general, this book is full of other people and events; it is full of voices of the Other. What we may find in each of the contributions to this collection is, to use Kostash's words, she who "stands as witness, and the story rewinds, and goes on, this time with her in attendance."[17] This time it is again the reader who, regardless of her cultural, ethnic, or national background, is encouraged to witness "the intimacies of overlapping histories"[18]: Ukrainian immigrants and their families in Toronto of the 1950s, internees in the Canadian First World War internment camps, Ukrainian Canadian-ness in Trudeau-era multiculturalism, *babas* living their harsh and hushed lives on the Canadian prairies, Ukrainian dissidents of the 1960s, journeys "home," medieval Christian martyrs, and nineteenth-century Indigenous rebels in Canada.

This book proves very well that the literary merit of Ukrainian Canadian writing can be appreciated by both Ukrainian Canadian and non–Ukrainian Canadian readers. Being located outside Canada, being a Polish researcher of Ukrainian Canadian literature, I can confirm the interest of the non–Ukrainian Canadian public in this writing. I do not mean here only my private and scholarly interest in the current status quo of English-language Ukrainian Canadian literature; what I mean is the enthusiasm for this literature (and Canadian literature as a whole) among other scholars and students that I witnessed during my studies at Greifswald University in Germany; what I mean is the growing interest in Ukrainian Canadian studies developed by universities in Ukraine; and, finally, what I mean is the passion and commitment that my colleagues and I inject into a Canadian Studies component at the English Department at Szczecin University in Poland so that Ukrainian Canadian literature can be known here.

The fact that the discussion about Ukrainian Canadian literature goes beyond the borders of Canada, marking increasingly its presence in a non–Ukrainian Canadian environment, allows me to finish here on a reassuring note. Grekul once wrote about the importance of "fostering ongoing dialogue about what it means to be Ukrainian and Canadian."[19] And while it *is* important for scholars of Ukrainian Canadian literature from "within" to engage with these identity issues, it is equally important for those from "outside" to do so. For we can rephrase Grekul's message as a statement of fact, a confirmation: Write your stories down – your voices *are* heard and also listened to!

NOTES

1 Some of the statements and ideas in this foreword have been taken from my doctoral dissertation "'*Za Hranetsiu*' – 'Beyond the Border,'" issued online by the Greifswald University Library in 2012.
2 Mycak, *Canuke Literature*, 94.
3 Ibid., 88.
4 Ibid., 81.
5 Cf. also Mycak's remarks on "generic confusion" (*Canuke Literature*, 88) or "generic hybridity" (89) in Ukrainian Canadian literature, which she also refers to as "a combination or intersection of discourses … [that] may be seen to externalise a discursive practice" (89), as "to a certain degree," Mycak confirms, "all texts are informed by other discourses and writers often conduct some form of research" (89).
6 Grekul, *Leaving Shadows*, xxiii. Italics in original.
7 Cf. also Grekul's conclusion, *Leaving Shadows*, 203.
8 Ibid., 203.
9 Kostash, "Writers Read; Readers Write," 62.
10 Mycak, *Canuke Literature*, 75.
11 Ibid., 79–95.
12 Such an understanding of a text and reading corresponds to post-structuralist ideas; for further information, see my discussion of Derrida, Fowler, and Hawthorn in my doctoral thesis, in Suchacka, "'*Za Hranetsiu*' – 'Beyond the Border,'" 382–3.
13 This observation is based on my understanding of Bakhtin's idea of "chronotope." For its analysis, see my doctoral thesis, "'*Za Hranetsiu*' – 'Beyond the Border,'" 384–5.
14 Ledohowski, "Canadian Cossacks," 26.
15 Ledohowski, "'I Am Enchanted,'" 138.
16 Ledohowski, "Canadian Cossacks," 37.
17 Kostash, "The Gulag, the Crypt, and the Gallows," 110.
18 Kostash, *The Doomed Bridegroom*, 110.
19 Grekul, *Leaving Shadows*, 199.

Acknowledgments

First and foremost we would like to express gratitude to Professors Lubomyr Luciuk and Robert Paul Magocsi, who envisioned this project as a way to commemorate both the 120th anniversary of the first permanent Ukrainian settlers to Canada and the 30th anniversary of the establishment of the Chair of Ukrainian Studies at the University of Toronto, in part by hosting a one-day symposium at the University of Toronto in 2011, out of which many of the contributions to this book grew. It is thanks to their initial vision, enthusiasm, encouragement, and funding that this project first came into being.

As well, we would like to thank the contributors to this volume. With only our promises and enthusiasm to offer them, we, the editors, were able to secure contributions and participation from excellent scholars and authors. They were patient with the delays that inevitably come with pulling together a publication of this sort, and they were generous with their time and insights. As well, Nightwood Editions and the House of Anansi generously granted permission for us to reprint poetry from Elizabeth Bachinsky and Erín Moure, respectively.

We gratefully acknowledge the support of the Ukrainian Studies Foundation, which provided financial backing for the early part of this project as a one-day symposium held in April 2011. We are also grateful to the Shevchenko Foundation, which provided us with a publication grant that allowed us to bring this book to fruition.

Our editor at University of Toronto Press, Siobhan McMenemy, has been a source of help and guidance through the process of bringing this book from submitted manuscript to finished product, and we cannot help but offer her our sincere thanks.

On a personal note, we would like to express just how much we enjoyed meeting and working with every one of the contributors to this book, those who joined this project right at the start and those we were fortunate enough to entice partway through the process. The contributors to this collection have been fun, challenging, creative, and professional at every turn; it has been a genuine pleasure to collaborate with such a strong group of writers and thinkers.

As no book can ever be produced without the patience and understanding of family and friends, partners and spouses, we give our thanks to Rueban and to Mike, and even to little Esmé. We look forward to the day when she is old enough to read this book!

Lisa Grekul & Lindy Ledohowski
2016

UNBOUND

Ukrainian Canadians Writing Home

Introduction: Ukrainian Canadian Poet Pedagogues

LINDY LEDOHOWSKI

People in general, love legends ... Such a legend has been spun around the arrival in Canada of the "two first" Ukrainian settlers, namely, Wasyl Elyniak and Ivan Pylypiw.

Michael Marunchak[1]

Wasyl Elyniak and Ivan Pylypiw are generally credited as having been the first Ukrainians to settle permanently in Canada, and while they may not have been the very first of Ukrainian descent to make the journey to Canada or to find their way to the Canadian wilds via other destinations,[2] their arrival in 1891 and settlement in Canada mark the beginning of sustained Ukrainian immigration to Canada and the growth and development of Ukrainian Canadian-ness in all its varied forms.

No fewer than 170,000 ethnic Ukrainians immigrated to Canada between 1896 and 1914. Vera Lysenko puts the number much higher, writing that "in fifteen years [Clifford Sifton's immigration policy] had brought two million immigrants from Eastern Europe." She believes there were 200,000 Ukrainians in Canada by 1908.[3] By 1900, approximately 16 per cent of all immigrants to Canada had come from the western Ukrainian province of Galicia.[4] After this first and largest wave of homesteading Ukrainians (1891–1914), around 68,000 Ukrainians immigrated to Canada between 1919 and 1939. During the third wave, between 1947 and 1952, a further 32,000 arrived,[5] most of them postwar displaced persons (DPs) – a Ukrainian urban intelligentsia different in many ways from the rural peasant émigrés who came before them.[6] Finally, the post-Soviet opening of former Eastern Bloc countries (like

Ukraine) has allowed for a fourth wave to begin. Some scholars date the beginning of this fourth wave even earlier. While the rate of immigration has slowed, currently more than one million Canadians identify themselves as Ukrainian (according to the most recent Canadian census). They settled across the Canadian prairies in bloc settlements; they settled in Canadian cities in ethnic ghettos; they also disappeared into the Canadian mosaic, blending into diverse communities and marrying non-Ukrainians. Regardless of their experience of immigration to and settlement in Canada, often they negotiate some kind of Ukrainian Canadian-ness, for in the words of Sonia Mycak, there are "subtle negotiations of identity which are still occurring two, three, four generations after the act of immigration."[7] All of these varied immigrants and their descendants make up a loose ethnocultural group of Ukrainian Canadians.

Often what this unbound group of so-called Ukrainian Canadians has in common is a kind of connection to Ukraine. For some it is a connection to the country itself as the country of one's birth before immigrating to Canada; for others it is a connection to Ukraine as an imagined ideal homeland where one's family stories originate; for some it is a connection to the Ukrainian language, politics, history; and for others still Ukraine represents the constantly deferred Derridean signifier – and it is that unbound variety and complexity of subject positions that fascinates.

This book does not offer a literary history or a survey of all Ukrainian Canadian literature in English; rather, it brings together a selection of voices that have been raised in the articulation of the many different faces of Ukrainian Canadian-ness since Elyniak and Pylypiw first came to Canada and decided to stay. In her comparative study of multiculturalisms, Sneja Gunew identifies what she calls "poet pedagogues"; these "artists who are also teachers" often "become the focus for creating and maintaining an intellectual community informed by the diasporic histories of its constituent members and enmeshed in contradictory relations with the dominant cultural paradigms."[8] There are many Ukrainian Canadian creative writers who also function as literary critics and ethnic theorists, as "poet pedagogues" communicating their individual visions of how best to retain, or address the loss of, Ukrainian Canadian-ness.

Over the past twenty-five years, a critical tradition has slowly been developing that sees Ukrainian Canadian English-language expression as a valid field of study in its own right, instead of merely the poor cousin of true Ukrainian Canadian literature written in Ukrainian.[9] There has long been a tradition of a small Ukrainian Canadian intelligentsia shaping the attitudes and beliefs of rank-and-file Ukrainian Canadians,[10] and a number of creative and critical writers in the growing English-language Ukrainian Canadian literary tradition fall into this category. In writing specifically about English-language Ukrainian Canadian writing, Mycak notes that "the author has become the site of identity and a new point of centrality from which the previously peripheral Canadian-Ukrainian [sic] voice now speaks."[11] These writings often show how and where the lines between the author, the scholar, the teacher, and the critic become blurred and intertwined.

Identities – ethnocultural, gendered, socio-economic, minoritized, regional – are interesting facets of who we are. Often we both are and are not multiple selves simultaneously, and as we asked authors to contribute to this collection, the key question we wanted them to think about was this: What does Ukrainian Canadian-ness mean to them in contemporary Canada? We were both surprised and pleased with their responses.

This book demonstrates that on close scrutiny, as with any vibrant and dynamic community, there may be more divisions than similarities among the views of individual Ukrainian Canadians. More than sixty years have passed since the first English-language Ukrainian Canadian novel was published, and the literature playing with notions of what it means to be Ukrainian Canadian suggests that it means many things to many people. This book explores the spaces where, in the words of Myrna Kostash, "our *collective*, though not necessarily common, interests coincide."[12] And while this exploration uses Ukrainian Canadian (in all its iterations) as its focusing lens, it speaks to other minoritized subject positions in Canada and abroad, and perhaps most loudly to contemporary mainstream Canada as well.

Pablo Picasso once said that "art is a lie that tells the truth," and these writers, artists, tell us many truths about Ukrainian-ness in today's Canada. As the starting point for this book, the following introduction offers a summary of some of the approaches that various "poet pedagogues" have taken with regard to what it means to be Ukrainian in Canada today, in order to map some of the terrain of the debates that many Ukrainian Canadian writers and critics have traversed. Of course, any sketch like this one necessarily smooths over wrinkles and possibly erases nuance, but I think the schema will help draw out points that the rest of this collection expresses and dramatizes with its many voices.

*

Position 1: "Ethnic" *Is* Canadian

Some of the writers who can be considered "poet pedagogues" who write about what it means to be both Ukrainian and Canadian are at pains to show that "Ukrainian-ness" must be understood as synonymous with "Canadian-ness." They argue that only by understanding how Ukrainian experiences are fundamental to Canadian experiences can we truly appreciate both. Two striking examples of this approach appear fifty years apart, and these authors are worthy of our attention. Both Vera Lysenko – whose non-fiction study of Ukrainian Canadians was published in 1947 and whose first novel was published in 1954 – and Lisa Grekul – whose non-fiction study of Ukrainian Canadian literature was published in 2005 and whose first novel was published in 2003 – situate their different analyses, expressed both critically and creatively, within a particular Canadian frame of reference. These authors' writings share more than a similar approach. Their critical works – Lysenko's *Men in Sheepskin Coats* and Grekul's *Leaving Shadows*, for instance – were preceded by essay collections on the same topic but are still seen as the "first" of their kind. William Paluk's *Canadian Cossacks* was published in 1942, five years before Lysenko's *Men in Sheepskin Coats*, but it does not offer the coherent, book-length analysis of Ukrainian Canadian history and experience that the latter does, and thus it is often overlooked. Recalling the relationship between Paluk's and Lysenko's works, Sonia Mycak's *Canuke Literature* was published in 2001, four years prior to Grekul's *Leaving Shadows*, but it is a collection of essays on Ukrainian Canadian fiction, not a complete, coherent account of Ukrainian Canadian literature like Grekul's text. So while neither Lysenko nor Grekul actually produced the first books on their topics, they are both generally accepted as having done so.[13]

And the similarities do not stop here. Lysenko wants to show how the Ukrainian experience is quintessentially Canadian, and Grekul wishes to demonstrate how Ukrainian Canadian literature in English is quintessentially Canadian. Put simply, Lysenko's main interest lies in explicating, historicizing, and describing Ukrainian Canadian presences and experiences as integral to Canada. Grekul's main interest, instead, lies in explicating, historicizing, and describing Ukrainian Canadian literature as integral to Canadian literary studies. Lysenko's non-fictional *Men in Sheepskin Coats* offers a history of Ukrainians in Canada, while Grekul's *Leaving Shadows* offers a literary history of Ukrainian Canadian writing. Nonetheless, both share a desire to bring Ukrainian materials – be they experiences and history or literary contributions – from a perceived position of marginality to one of centrality. For each author, Canada, as a nation or national literature, functions as the imagined construct to which they append Ukrainian-ness.

Lysenko's stated aim in writing *Men in Sheepskin Coats* is "to show how the destiny of the Men in Sheepskin Coats [Ukrainians] was bound up with the destiny of Canada";[14] she wants to write Ukrainian Canadians onto Canada's centre stage. With a related goal, Grekul notes: "The Ukrainian Canadian literary tradition simply will not survive if it is not included in classroom syllabi and drawn into ongoing debates in Canadian literary studies ... The challenge for Ukrainian Canadian literary scholars – which mirrors that of early feminist and postcolonial scholars – is how to incorporate this 'marginal' body of literature into the mainstream";[15] she wants to write (and teach) Ukrainian Canadian literature onto Canadian literature's centre stage. Both see proselytizing as key to their intellectual projects.

Lysenko and Grekul both conceive of the Canadian nation as the foundation on which their analyses are built. Lysenko views Canada as a nation growing into greatness and thus has written a book showing how Ukrainian Canadians participated in this larger project and continue to do so. Grekul views Canadian literature as developing from a more homogeneous "former British colony" to a "post-national community increasingly defined by the diasporic consciousness of many members,"[16] and thus has written a book showing how Ukrainian Canadian literature follows this development. If Smaro Kamboureli is correct that "the kind of anxiety that has continued to characterize both what Canadian literature is and what constitutes Canadian identity" is "particularly Canadian,"[17] then the fixation with and anxiety about Ukrainian Canadian literature and what constitutes Ukrainian Canadian identity are also "particularly Canadian," and this is exactly the point that both Lysenko and Grekul wish to make.

Position 2: I'm Not "Ethnic"!

When Ukrainian Canadian English-language writing really began to come to the fore in the 1970s and 1980s,[18] the idea of being a representative "ethnic" or "Ukrainian" writer was something that many authors rejected outright. For instance, so-called Ukrainian Canadian writers such as Maara Haas and George Ryga were adamant that they did not consider themselves "ethnic." At a conference on ethnicity and writing in Canada held in 1979 in Alberta, both were vocal about their distaste for the focus on Ukrainian-ness and ethnicity in relation to them as people, and as writers. Haas said, "It takes great discipline on my part not to vomit when I hear the word ethnic." She emphasized how even a discussion of marginalized ethnic sensibilities (which was one of the conference's purposes) privileges the non-ethnic: "Each time the word ethnic rears its hyphenated head, the odour of a clogged sewer smelling of racism poisons the air." She considered herself an "unhyphenated Canadian writer."[19] Ryga spoke after Haas and was in full agreement with her. He told the audience, "I find it difficult to see myself as a so-called hyphenated Canadian," and he suggested that the "translation of bohunk into Ukrainian Canadian" is to "settle for something slightly nicer but equally harmful."[20] Many other Ukrainian Canadians – whether they are authors or not – share those views and see any discussion of either "Canadian-ness" or "Ukrainian-ness" as simply reiterating destructive power dynamics, the "vertical mosaic" that John Porter theorized.[21]

It is now commonplace in multiculturalism studies in Canada to point to how the dynamics of multiculturalism create binaries that reinforce mainstream versus marginalized dynamics.[22] Eva Mackey makes a compelling argument along these lines, clarifying how the logic of contemporary Canadian multiculturalism has created two categories of ethnic identities – multicultural or hyphenated Canadians (ethnic ones) and mainstream or Canadian Canadians (non-ethnic ones).[23] Writers like Haas and Ryga oppose the inclusionary rhetoric of multicultural policies – rhetoric that in fact tries to keep people pigeonholed into categories they may very well reject. In line with these views, Helen Potrebenko, the author of *No Streets of Gold* (1977), a study of Ukrainian immigration to the Canadian prairies, rails against the insistence that she be considered a Ukrainian Canadian writer: "I wish to be defined as a writer without the various hyphens." She wrote: "I took a copy of *No Streets of Gold* to a used bookstore – the proprietor said happily: Oh good, there's always a market for Canadian history."[24] She sighed with relief at the bookseller's conception of her as the author of a book of Canadian history, no hyphens.

So Lysenko seeks "to preserve something of [Ukrainian] origins,"[25] and Grekul seeks to foster "ongoing dialogue about what it means to be Ukrainian and Canadian,"[26] indicating their continued investment in "Ukrainian-ness" by showing its importance to "Canadian-ness"; whereas writers like Haas, Ryga, and Potrebenko refuse any

"Ukrainian" labelling, which they see as nothing more than contributing to an ongoing process of minoritization.

Position 3: Picking Up My "Ethnic" Baggage

For some authors, teachers, and everyday Ukrainian Canadians, the question about the "Ukrainian" part of their ethnic identity is no question at all. Their ethnocultural heritage is as much a part of who they are as their eye colour or their height. For instance, Marsha Forchuk Skrypuch has said that she has "written more works of fiction with a Ukrainian theme than anyone else in Canada"[27] and been widely celebrated as an author of young adult historical fiction. Many of her works deal with Ukrainian and Ukrainian Canadian experiences. As the descendant of a survivor of Canada's First World War internment camps in which more than 5,000 Canadians of Ukrainian heritage were interned, Skrypuch has never ignored her ethnic identity; but at the same time, it has carried with it complications and shame. Part of working through the sense of inherited shame at her "Ukrainian-ness" took the form of her literary output, and she has been one of the most prolific voices on the Ukrainian Canadian landscape. By reaching schoolchildren as a "poet pedagogue," she has had a profound impact on the next generation. Skrypuch has never seemed to question her Ukrainian Canadian identity, whereas other writers reject outright the idea of belonging to a Ukrainian identity in Canada (e.g., Haas, Ryga, Potrebenko). Then there are authors whose views about their "Ukrainian-ness" have changed over time. Janice Kulyk Keefer is an interesting Ukrainian Canadian writer in the context of this shifting approach to identity: her own views regarding her ethnic identity have changed throughout her career as a writer. She charts this shift in her 1995 essay "Coming Across Bones: Historiographic Ethnofiction," in which she writes that

> by the time I left to enter university, I had decided to remove myself as far as possible from the claustrophobia and painfully split subjectivity induced by my experience of ethnicity. I decided to study English literature; I married outside the Ukrainian community – an Anglik, or Englishman, as he was referred to by friends of my family ... I went to England to do graduate studies and became an arch-Anglophile; I even developed an English accent, which, I must have believed, would cure that ragged split in my tongue.[28]

She continues: "I have various explanations for my recalcitrance vis-à-vis 'writing ethnicity,'" not the least of which was to avoid being "pigeonholed as an ethnic writer, someone whose work would only be of interest to a small community of 'like-blooded' readers."[29] Yet despite this decision early in her career to distance herself from her ethnic Ukrainian roots, she writes in this essay that she has "finally returned to claim that baggage" of her ethnicity.[30] She has expressed her reclaiming of that baggage in a number of ways, from academic articles on ethnicity generally and Ukrainian Canadian ethnicity specifically, to novels, to a lecture series, to her travel memoir outlining her first journey "back" to a Ukraine she had never seen. So in the 1970s and 1980s, Kulyk Keefer, like many other Ukrainian Canadian writers, did not want to be considered "ethnic," but by the 1990s something had changed for her, and her "Ukrainian-ness" had become a significant element in her professional output as a writer.

Likewise, Marusya Bociurkiw admits to having disowned her Ukrainian ethnic baggage in the 1990s, only to return to it later, as an adult prepared to deal with hearing the telling and retelling of her grandmother's traumatic story of immigration.[31] In her 2006 novel *The Children of Mary*, the protagonist is a Ukrainian Canadian and the setting is the Ukrainian community in North End Winnipeg.[32] And her preface to her 2007 memoir *Comfort Food for Breakups* specifically situates the reader side by side with her in a specifically Ukrainian Canadian context: "You're kissed profusely on both cheeks, immediately led by hand into the kitchen, and pushed into a chair (rather brusquely) at the head of a yellow formica table. Then, without much conversation, Evhenia Wasylyshyn, nee Protskiv, born in a small village in Western Ukraine in 1903, and long since exiled to Edmonton, will get to work."[33] The image, using second person pronouns, draws us into her *baba*'s kitchen, making us participants in the "Ukrainian-ness" enveloped within.

Yet neither Kulyk Keefer nor Bociurkiw understands "Ukrainian-ness" in simplified celebratory terms. As they reclaim their ethnic baggage, both find themselves working through the problematic elements of Ukrainian anti-Semitism: Kulyk Keefer writes passionately about her growing realization that "Jewish–Ukrainian relations are as complicated as they are traumatic,"[34] and Bociurkiw believes that "Ukraine bears a heavy burden of complicity with anti-Semitism" and that "its history of pogroms has yet to be fully acknowledged and documented, let alone worked through."[35] Their return to reclaim their Ukrainian baggage requires them to acknowledge its uncomfortable weight.

While Haas, Ryga, and Potrebenko never explicitly return to "claim that baggage," I have argued elsewhere that their texts demonstrate attention to "Ukrainian-ness" however much they protest otherwise. "By the 1980s," I contend, "they produced works contributing to a developing sense of Ukrainian-hyphen-Canadianness."[36] While these authors never openly or dramatically declare themselves "Ukrainian" or "Ukrainian Canadian," both Kulyk Keefer and Bociurkiw do. This book explores what each author – as both critic and creative writer – has to say about being Ukrainian Canadian today.

Position 4: What Is Ukrainian-ness Anyway?

By now, the examples of Lysenko, Grekul, Haas, Ryga, Potrebenko, Skrypuch, Kulyk Keefer, and Bociurkiw should demonstrate just how varied some of the views of these authors are when it comes to articulating what "Ukrainian-ness" in a Canadian context means to them. One of the most important writers in this English-language oeuvre is Myrna Kostash, and her relationship to her own Ukrainian Canadian heritage is even more multifaceted. While she never rejected her so-called ethnic past (she openly wrote "that Ukrainians have been drunks and criminals, anti-Semites and wife-batterers,"[37] demonstrating her resistance to a glorified imagining of "Ukrainian-ness"), it was not until she turned her journalistic attention to Ukrainian settlement on the prairies in 1977 that she found herself emerging as a "kind of spokesperson in western Canada for the idea of ethnicity."[38] But this new position exposed her to many more questions than answers about her relationship to Ukrainian or Ukrainian Canadian ethnic identities: "How is ethnicity inherited without the language or the literature? ... Am I ethnic because I wrote about Ukrainians or is there something else about me in my function as a writer which is ethnic? The question for me, then, is did I write that book as an ethnic or as a journalist?"[39] She began to wonder: "What *is* ethnicity? How is it related to being a western Canadian? Is it a source of strength or is it debilitating in the modern world? How can I be an ethnic and a feminist at the same time? How does my ethnicity affect my writing?"[40] In some ways, these sorts of questions about a Ukrainian ethnic identity – in relation to both Canada and Ukraine – have continued to play important roles in much of Kostash's post-1977 writing. She has continued to explore various facets of "Ukrainian-ness," asking new questions: "Who are the Ukrainian Canadians who come after me, after deficit slashing and program extermination, after webnets and the Coca-Colonization of everything, after Ukrainian independence and *Koka-Kola* on the sidewalks and cafes of Kyiv? How does one go on being Ukrainian Canadian in *their* world? Does it still matter, in the so-called global village, that hyphen is a kind of hinge between two equally compelling identities?"[41]

For more than thirty years, Kostash has been actively engaged in asking these kinds of questions about what it means to be Ukrainian *and* Canadian. Her ethnic baggage was never deposited off to the side; it is a source of ongoing curiosity to her. And she compares her own ethnic experiences to those of other so-called Ukrainian Canadians of later generations, writers such as Elizabeth Bachinsky, Daria Salamon, and Lisa Grekul.

For instance, Grekul's work as both a scholar and a writer has been strongly influenced by Kostash. We can read Grekul's first novel, in some ways, as a fictional follow-up to Kostash's 1977 sociological study of Ukrainian immigration to the Canadian prairies, *All of Baba's Children*. Set in the same Two Hills area of Alberta, Grekul's narrative presents a protagonist born around the time that Kostash's book was first published who grapples with the ethnic legacy outlined in Kostash's non-fiction work. Grekul's Colleen is the descendent of hard-working Ukrainian immigrants, like the peasant farmers who homesteaded and settled the Canadian prairie, the second-generation of whom Kostash interviewed for her book. Moreover, Grekul claims that the mere existence of Kostash's study influenced her developmental years as "everyone in my family bought a copy of it."[42] She also writes that her novel provides a response to *All of Baba's Children*; she "set out to write the Great Ukrainian Canadian novel"[43] because she was "convinced at that point that there was no Ukrainian Canadian literature in English."[44] For Grekul, Ukrainian Canadian-ness is always in development and is best managed by the production of Ukrainian Canadian texts. While Kostash may ask what Ukrainian Canadian-ness will look like for the generations that follow her, Grekul suggests that the answers to such questions will be meted out in the pages of literary works. She finds the most hope in Ukrainian Canadian texts that "emphasize the notion that reinvention is the key to maintaining ties to their ethnic roots ... Writing [that] is less about coming home than about the open-ended, perpetual search for home."[45] In her view, this kind of openness relates directly to "Canadian literary studies" as "a space where the relation between ethnic minority literatures, multicultural ideology, and mainstream literary culture is already hotly debated" and where there is room for more "work on Ukrainian Canadian literary texts."[46] Kostash, by contrast, asks questions about "Ukrainian-ness" in a variety of open contexts.

The very title of an interview with Grekul, Gunew, and Margery Fee, "Myrna Kostash: Ukrainian Canadian Non-Fiction Prairie New Leftist Feminist Canadian Nationalist,"[47] draws attention to the multiple identities inherent in Kostash's questioning.

She is not alone in her multiplicity of identities, in being unbound by categorizations. In fact, all of the authors who have contributed to this book ask questions about envisioning a Ukrainian Canadian identity that is highly contextual, informed by particular places, and shaped by both the larger currents of geopolitical trends and the smaller details of familial dynamics.

Position 5: Nationalists versus Communists

This introduction has surveyed the various ways that authors and critics have tackled the complicated questions relating to "Ukrainian-ness" in Canada. It would be remiss of me at this point not to mention the backdrop for Ukrainian Canadian literature and studies throughout the twentieth century. For most of that century, Ukraine was locked behind the Iron Curtain. Among Ukrainians in Canada, the absorption of Ukraine into a larger Socialist empire produced two diametrically opposed attitudes: for some, questions of Ukrainian national independence took precedence; for others, questions of socialist solidarity were most important. Frances Swyripa in *Wedded to the Cause* identifies these two main groups of Ukrainian Canadians as the nationalists and the progressives.[48] The nationalists viewed Ukrainian Canadian issues mainly in terms of the historic struggle for Ukrainian independence; the progressives, in terms of broader socio-economic concerns.

Ukraine had been independent for twenty years by the time of the 2011 symposium that launched this project. Obviously, Ukrainian independence affects Ukrainians in Canada very differently today than during the Soviet era, when it had yet to be achieved. In recent decades, Ukrainian Canadian concerns have been less about a grand socialist collective in which Soviet Ukraine plays a part and less about a tireless struggle to lift the Soviet yoke from Ukrainian shoulders. At the same time, contemporary debates and conflicts about how close Ukraine should be to the so-called West or Russia replay some of the earlier, Soviet-era dynamics.

*

Ukrainian politics in Ukraine have been shaped by a perceived binary between the West and Russia – an overly simplistic view that ignores and erases the agency of Ukrainians themselves and the plurality of Ukrainian identities on the territory of Ukraine itself. *A Short History of Tractors in Ukrainian* author Marina Lewycka writes in the contemporary context that we should be wary of embracing this too simple version of the West versus Russia played out across the Ukrainian landscape, in which Ukrainians are viewed as mere "pawns in a cynical east-west power game of spheres of influence" – something that she laments has little "to do with the wellbeing and happiness of ordinary people."[49]

In 2004, the pro-Russian presidential candidate, Viktor Yanukovych, won the election in Ukraine by a narrow margin. The result of that election spurred widespread protests and claims of electoral fraud among citizens and international observers. Those protests, now known as the Orange Revolution (the incident Bachinsky refers to in her chapter of this book), saw the elections declared null. Now, during the publication process for this book on what it means to be Ukrainian in Canada today, Ukraine has been thrust into an ever worsening crisis.

The autumn of 2013 saw things come to a head in Ukraine with the Euromaidan protests in central Kiev, during which hundreds of thousands of Ukrainians filled *maidans* (squares) to protest government corruption and push Ukraine towards greater EU integration. Now the global community watches as war bleeds Ukraine. The contributors to this book had been asked what it means to be Ukrainian in Canada today; sadly, that question has taken on a more painful and poignant tone over the course of preparing this collection. We have been asked by our communities, by our students, by our friends, by our families, by our colleagues, and most certainly by ourselves, what our responses are to the conflict in Ukraine. And our responses are varied. This introduction cannot summarize for a lay person what the root causes of the current conflict are, nor can it predict the fate of Ukraine going forward. However, this book in its entirety offers an invitation to think about our positions not just as members of a Ukrainian diaspora but also as Canadians and global citizens.

As this traumatic war in Ukraine continues to rage, Ukrainian Canadians see the questions they have long been asking writ large in a new and agonizing context: What does it mean to be Ukrainian? What is the role of Ukrainian nationalism? What is or should be the relationship between Ukraine and Russia? What is or should be the relationship between Ukraine and the West? What is the role of Ukrainians abroad? Of their descendants? What can we do?

Ukrainian Canadian communities have by no means been unified in their answers to these sorts of questions, in the past *or* the present. In the words of Kulyk Keefer, the hyphen joining Ukrainian and Canadian provides "a connecting of elements or beings that possess as many differences between them as similarities ... And while in some ways the hyphen in our identity can be as silken and soft as a ribbon, it can also act as a sliver under the skin, or as a vivid scar marking the infliction of a wound."[50] The various approaches the writers anthologized here have held offer evidence of the wide-ranging sentiments regarding how "Ukrainian-ness" in Canada has been constructed.

For all of the contributors this book, whatever ethnicity, Ukrainian-ness, or Ukrainian Canadian-ness may signify to them, discourses of identity vis-à-vis national identity have been significant – more so now than ever – as war continues to explode in Ukraine.

Not insignificantly, all of the contributors to this book are women, as are the co-editors. This was not by design, but it is not without import. In their introduction to *Sisters or Strangers*, a collection of essays looking specifically at gender and immigration in Canada, the authors write that "one woman's experience of becoming 'Canadian' might be very different from another's and as such, questions of *difference* are as important to understanding immigrant women's lives as are questions of *commonality*."[51] This book collects the differing voices of daughters of immigrants, and it is worth noting that Ukrainian women – *babas* and their descendants – have long featured prominently in Ukrainian Canadian literature in English. That is not to say there are no male Ukrainian Canadian authors, because there certainly are: George Ryga, Andrew Suknaski, Ted Galay, Danny Schur, and Larry Warwaruk, to name a few. However, Ukrainian Canadian literature regularly focuses on female characters. Often this oeuvre features "young, female protagonists engaged in complex cultural and personal negotiations with their *babas*."[52] The importance of female characters and symbolism in Ukrainian Canadian literature in English may well have a link to Ukraine itself. For example, in writing about the importance of female symbolism in Ukraine, Marian Rubchak asserts that "female centrality remains lodged as an idea in the Ukrainian psyche."[53] Ukrainian mothers asked their soldier sons not to stop the protesters gathered on the Euromaidan – a story that garnered international attention.[54] Even the statue atop the column in the middle of Kiev's Independence Square – the heart of the Euromaidan protests – is a *Berehynia*, an embodiment of a kind of feminized Ukrainian nationalism in the person of a hearth mother and pagan goddess figure. Gender and ethnocultural identities, therefore, are not so neatly untangled if a persistent feminized *topos* underlies a kind of Ukrainian-ness. The contributors to this book alternately unravel and weave together the strands comprising their ethnocultural and gendered identities, creating characters and personae that are mothers and lovers and daughters and granddaughters, moving beyond essentialist femaleness to complex and dynamic feminisms.

This literary sisterhood does not offer one single answer to questions about Ukrainian Canadian-ness; these writers suggest there are many ways of shaping, articulating, and defining this particular ethnic subject position. These "poet pedagogues" are profoundly literary, and they muse on their own positions as they pertain to both writing and ethnicity, but rather than embark on a surgical process, scalpel in hand, trying to cut away this or that part of themselves to try to hold up individual bits for examination, they show the interconnectedness of their many different identities. These authors suggest that in examining the whole – with its contradictions, its complications, and its exciting elements – something real and something powerful may be glimpsed.

Their exploration, moreover, does not follow straightforward generic lines and boundaries; just as their identities are multiple, mutable, and in flux, so do their approaches wend and wind through methodologies that are both/neither critical/creative. In questioning notions of a creative-critical binary, Fred Wah has written that he has "always enjoyed writing poetry as a way of reading and thinking." In his words, "the language and methods of poetry have always seemed right to me; they push at the boundaries of thinking; they play in the noise and excess of language; they upset and they surprise. To write critically I've always written poetry."[55] The selections gathered here embody this notion: the poetic is critical, and the critical is poetic.

English Studies in Canada, the scholarly journal distributed to every member of the Association of Canadian College and University Teachers of English, recently published a special edition focused on the forms and practices shaping scholarly English discourse. Many of the articles responded to Stephen Slemon's question "Why Do I Have to Write Like that?"[56] with a call for a broader understanding of scholarly discourse in the field of literary studies. The selections in this book often challenge the given assumptions of a scholarly paper. While some of the pieces seem to fit the expected form – complete with footnotes and scholarly vocabulary – others at times become poetic or confessional. The authors in this collection trust the reader to respond not just to *what* they have to say about contemporary identity politics as writers in Canada, but also to *how* they choose to say it. The "unbound" of our title, therefore, refers to being unbound by the traditional rules of genre, by the expectations of "scholarly" prose, by rigid rules dictating identity allegiances, by lines dictating who can or cannot speak as "Ukrainian Canadian," and by traditional chains linking language proficiency to ethnic identity.

The first chapter, "Language Lessons" by Janice Kulyk Keefer, offers intimate insights into the notion of being "betwixt and between." For Kulyk Keefer, this sense of in-between-ness creates a personal instability that, ironically, has become a great sense of strength and insight for her as a writer. Not part of either the early wave of homesteading Ukrainian immigrants or the later politicized DPs arriving in Canada after the Second World War, she writes about feeling alienated from what Ukrainian Canadian discourse defined for her as her identity. She grapples with the notion of language – the Ukrainian language – and her struggles to master it, to embrace it. For her, it is in the position of being poised at the nexus of more than one culture and language that she finds connectivity; in this sense of disconnect she finds commonality. She closes with a poem of a mother and child on a bus, trying to connect.

Chapter 2 offers Elizabeth Bachinsky's personal prose insights as a prologue to her long poem "The Wax Ceremony." Bachinsky's familial roots may be in Saskatchewan, but she grew up in British Columbia, separated from the sense of a prairie-based "Ukrainian-ness" that many of the descendants of those early homesteaders enjoyed. Her selection here presents the contemporary writer engaging with the subject of her past and the need to learn about Ukrainian and Ukrainian Canadian history. She invites us into the question "How could I continue to claim a heritage without having any sense of the history?" Through the motif of the writer at her desk, we find these snippets of history. The poem is expansive in its treatment of the internment of Ukrainian Canadians during the First World War,[57] but when she comes to the famine-genocide, the Ukrainian *Holodomor*,[58] all she can say is that "She can't begin to write / about this"; the trauma and the suffering are beyond words, beyond expression. While this chapter conveys some of Bachinsky's own feelings about articulating Ukrainian-ness as she researched and wrote her Ukrainian-themed collection of poetry, *God of Missed Connections*, the following chapter follows young adult author Marsha Forchuk Skrypuch's confessional journey to find her own voice as a writer. Her personal essay charts her journey into writing as a way of connecting; like Kulyk Keefer, she finds a sense of non-belonging to be a powerful driving force behind her writing and her inquiries into what it means to be Ukrainian, or more precisely, what it means to be a Ukrainian Canadian writer, reaching children and young adults. In many ways, her reach into their classrooms makes her one of the most important "poet pedagogues" gathered here.

From Skrypuch's personal confessional piece, the book moves to critic, writer, and film-maker Marusya Bociurkiw, the daughter of Ukrainian immigrants, who grew up in a highly politicized Ukrainian Canadian home. She theorizes both the writing and the reception of her memoir *Comfort Food for Breakups*. In a kind of free verse poem, Bociurkiw mingles art with identity with food. She tells us that "food and hospitality speak where words cannot," and in both her silences and her descriptions she takes us into a community that is both inclusive and pained. Bociurkiw adds to her earlier writing with reflections on her contemporary trips to Ukraine as the Euromaidan protests, the revolution, and armed conflict erupt. She offers a powerful witnessing of the struggles of Ukrainians in this contemporary moment.

In chapter 5, Montreal poet Erín Moure offers a prose musing on her trips to Ukraine to connect with and discover her own mother's natal home. In the past, Moure's poetry had very little to do with her mother's Ukrainian heritage; she was interested, rather, in exploring language and how it works, a concern that she carries forward here. Her multilingual prose and poetic chapter expresses some of the complicated ways in which Ukrainian-ness is inextricably linked with other identities, most notably Jewish-ness and Polish-ness. One image she describes is of a photograph of her mother as a young child with a Polish name taken by a Jewish man who did not survive the Holocaust. This photographic artefact is then given to the Canadian Moure in contemporary Ukraine. This Polish-Jewish-Ukrainian-Canadian piece of the past given to Moure in the present is one of the greatest gifts of her journey "home." Like Kulyk Keefer, who thinks about ethnic identity in specifically linguistic terms, Moure switches from English to French to Ukrainian with ease, foregrounding the interplay among her multiple selves. Her selection ends with a poetic excerpt from *The Unmemntioable*, building on this sense of the power of words and language to create and articulate identity and selfhood in all its complications and contradictions. Chapter 6 offers a bit of levity as novelist Daria Salamon meditates on the progression that saw her book become *more* not *less*

Ukrainian as a publishing strategy. This process brought her to realize that her Ukrainian-ness is something worth celebrating, not in a trite way, but simply because it is who she is. She, like Skrypuch, focuses intently on the relationship linking Ukrainian Canadian-ness to writing and readers' expectations.

Chapter 7 belongs to Myrna Kostash, who writes about her own relationship to ethnicity as mediated through sexuality and eroticism. In particular, she offers a metatextual musing on three of her recent publications that examine the relationship between the erotic and the political and how that relationship has shaped her own understanding of Ukraine. She writes about three male hero characters who have peopled some of her previous books; for her, the landscape of political dissidence is more of a shared terrain than the simple language of ethnocultural identity. She writes about writing and the indeterminate nature of truth and how the written word – the play with genre – becomes both the land and language to think about and work through the subject of selfhood.

The concluding section brings these offerings together, demonstrating the ways in which, gender, sexuality, ethnicity, and language function in concert with the writer's own imagination and sensibility, and offering summative observations as Grekul weaves together the many threads that each contributor has provided. Important to note, as well, is that the medium for literature and its attendant discourse has evolved over time, with the authors here engaging with social media. The immediacy of digital sharing offers a powerful tool for connecting. Famously, Walter Benjamin examined the role of technology in creating and affecting art and artistic representation in a world in which art can be reproduced infinitely.[59] Today, social media sites like Facebook take these insights further than Benjamin could have anticipated, situating infinite reproducibility and near-infinite dissemination in the exact temporal moment of creation. Facebook and sites like it also, however, have the power to demand immediate and real-time responses from "poet pedagogues," a dynamic that Lisa Grekul's conclusion to this collection theorizes.

This book provides an appendix listing the many English-language creative texts written by Ukrainian Canadians about Ukrainian Canadians since the publication of Vera Lysenko's *Yellow Boots*, the first novel in English by a Canadian of Ukrainian descent. This bibliography offers readers a glimpse of fifty-five years of English-language Ukrainian Canadian writing. This is a book, therefore, for and by writers, but it is also deeply and profoundly a book for readers. It is both a confession and an invitation.

Make no mistake, identity – Ukrainian-ness in its many guises – haunts these writers. In the words of Kulyk Keefer, "it is the work of artists able to raise those ghosts for us, and to make us look them in the face, that we must encourage and reward with our heightened, exacting attention."[60] This book presents these ghosts, complicated, conflicted, and contradictory as they may be, because in looking them in the face, so to speak, we bring them to light. And only through this frank and public confrontation may we find points of connection. As Kostash writes, it is "in the public sphere" that "our *collective* if not common interests coincide."[61]

NOTES

1 Marunchak, *The Ukrainian Canadians*, 23.
2 In a footnote to *Men in Sheepskin Coats*, her 1947 historical survey of Ukrainian immigration and settlement in Canada, Vera Lysenko notes the prior presence of at least three Ukrainian émigrés whose lives are now lost to history, 6.
3 Lysenko, *Men in Sheepskin Coats*, 32, 64.
4 Marunchak gives these numbers, noting that out of the 41,681 total new immigrants, 6,618 were from Galicia (Marunchak, *The Ukrainian Canadians*, 46).
5 I have used the generally accepted figures in providing this background. For more information, see Balan, *Salt and Braided Bread*; Ewanchuk, *Pioneer Profiles*; Grekul, *Leaving Shadows*; Hlynka, *The Other Canadians*; Hryniuk and Luciuk, *Canada's Ukrainians*; Lupul, *A Heritage in Transition*; Martynowych, *Ukrainians in Canada*; and Marunchak, *The Ukrainian Canadians*.
6 In the post–Second World War years, "displaced persons" (DPs) referred to those who were unable (or unwilling) to be repatriated to their country of origin; they were placed in camps and ultimately sent to resettle elsewhere. Between 1946 and 1952, some 165,000 DPs arrived in Canada; around 32,000 of them were of Ukrainian origin.
7 Mycak, *Canuke Literature*, 47.
8 Gunew, *Haunted Nations*, 13.
9 See Balan and Klynovy, "Introduction," xviii; Mycak, *Canuke Literature*, xi; Klymasz, Review of *Prairie Fire*, 163; Grekul, *Leaving Shadows*, xvii–xix.
10 Stebelsky, "The Resettlement," 148; Woycenko, *The Ukrainians in Canada*, 15.

11 Mycak, *Canuke Literature*, 94.
12 Kostash, *All of Baba's Great Grandchildren*, 37.
13 See Mycak, *Canuke Literature*, 1; Padolsky, "Canadian Ethnic Minority Literature," 363; Grekul, *Leaving Shadows*, 33–46; and Balan and Klynovy, "Introduction," xviii.
14 Lysenko, *Men in Sheepskin Coats*, 3.
15 Grekul, *Leaving Shadows*, 203.
16 Ibid., xix.
17 Smaro Kamboureli, "Introduction," 6.
18 Padolsky, "Canadian Ethnic Minority Literature," 364; Kirtz, "Old World Traditions," 8; Grekul, *Leaving Shadows*, xv.
19 Maara Haas, quoted in Balan, *Identifications*, 136.
20 George Ryga, quoted in Balan, *Identifications*, 141.
21 Porter, *The Vertical Mosaic*.
22 Moodley, "Canadian Multiculturalism as Ideology."
23 Mackey, *The House of Difference*, 3.
24 Potrebenko, Review of *Leaving Shadows*, 100.
25 Lysenko, *Men in Sheepskin Coats*, 4.
26 Grekul, *Leaving Shadows*, 199.
27 Marsha Forchuk Skrypuch, e-mail message to author, 4 March 2011.
28 Kulyk Keefer, "Coming Across Bones," 87–8.
29 Ibid., 89.
30 Ibid., 89.
31 Bociurkiw, "Bordercrossings," 6.
32 Bocirkiw, *The Children of Mary*, 27.
33 Ibid., 13.
34 Kulyk Keefeer, "Coming Across Bones," 87.
35 Bociurkiw, *Comfort Food for Breakups*, 26.
36 Ledohowski, "Becoming the Hyphen," 122.
37 Kostash, *All of Baba's Children*, xiv.
38 Kostash, "The Shock of White Cognition," 4.
39 Myrna Kostash, quoted Balan, *Identifications*, 137, 138.
40 Kostash, *All of Baba's Children*, xv.
41 Kostash, *All of Baba's Great Grandchildren*, 12–13.
42 Grekul, *Leaving Shadows*, ix.
43 Grekul, "Re-placing Ethnicity: Literature in English," 5.
44 Wawryshyn, interview with Lisa Grekul, 8.
45 Grekul, *Leaving Shadows*, 201.
46 Grekul, "Re-placing Ethnicity: New Approaches," 380.
47 Fee, Gunew, and Grekul, "Myrna Kostash."

48 Swyripa, *Wedded to the Cause.*
49 Lewycka, "Ukraine and the West."
50 Kulyk Keefer, *Dark Ghost*, 21, 22.
51 Epp, Iacovetta, and Swyripa, *Sisters or Strangers?*, 6.
52 Ledohowski, "Little Ukraine on the Prairie," 191.
53 Rubchak, "Ukraine's Ancient Matriarch," 132.
54 Sridharan, "Kiev Protests."
55 Wah, *Faking It*, 6.
56 Slemon, "Why Do I Have to Write Like That?"
57 Under the War Measures Act of 1914, approximately 5,000 Canadians of Ukrainian descent were interned in various concentration camps throughout Canada during the First World War. In 2005, Bill C-331, the Internment of Persons of Ukrainian Origin Recognition Act (the Ukrainian Canadian Restitution Act), which recognized this unjust internment, was passed. In May 2008, funds were allocated for various projects to commemorate the internment of Ukrainian Canadians. The Canadian First World War Internment Recognition Council began its activities in 2009; these included unveiling one hundred plaques across Canada in 2014 to memorialize the hundredth anniversary of this internment. For more information on this redress campaign, see Kordan and Mahovsky, *A Bare and Impolitic Right*; Kordan and Melnycky, *In the Shadow of the Rockies*; Kordan, *Enemy Aliens*; Luciuk, *Without Just Cause*; and Luciuk, *Righting an Injustice.*
58 The *Holodomor* was the genocide-by-famine of millions of Ukrainians in 1932 and 1933 under Josef Stalin's collectivization policies. The Canadian Parliament recognized it as a genocide in 2003. For information on the *Holodomor*, see Chamberlain, *The Ukraine*, 60–1; Kolasky, *Education in Soviet Ukraine*, 20; Manning, *The Story of the Ukraine*, 282; Manning, *Twentieth-Century Ukraine*, 93; and Subtelny, *Ukraine*, 413–16, 529.
59 Benjamin, "The Work of Art."
60 Kulyk Keefer, *Dark Ghost*, 51.
61 Kostash, *All of Baba's Great Grandchildren*, 37.

1 Language Lessons

JANICE KULYK KEEFER

Ni te, ni se: an adequate translation of "betwixt and between." What I love in the English is the bristling effect of the letters – in "betwixt," especially, I see that forest of long, twisted thorns and bare branches through which Prince Charming fought to reach Sleeping Beauty. The Ukrainian words would seem to mean "not this, not that," a far more pallid affair – as opposed to, for example, the word for "tenderness," *neezhneest'*, with *neezh*, the word for "knife," slipped beside the other letters like a blade into a sheath.

Wordplay – how appropriate a way to begin for a poet pedagogue, if that is what I am – for I do write poetry and I do teach.[1] I might as well own up right away, at least as far as my poet-credentials are concerned: language for me is the defining characteristic of my Ukrainian-ness, which I experience as something conflicted, problematic, endlessly engaging. I don't feel myself to be "naturally" Ukrainian, as a good friend of mine does. Neither she nor I were born there; we did not grow up there; we have never lived there, as opposed to being visitors, and yet, because she spent her first eighteen years or so in a home where it was forbidden to speak anything but Ukrainian, and because her parents, both of them displaced persons, or DPs, bred in her a burning love for the homeland she had never known, she declares herself to be as much Ukrainian as she is American (she was born in New Jersey) or Canadian (she has lived in Toronto for the past thirty years).

It's because I can't speak Ukrainian with any fluency, as well as because I was raised to think of myself as Canadian before anything else, that I lay no claim to being an *Ukrainka*. Yet neither do I feel Ukrainian Canadian in any conventional way: I don't belong to any community organization; I don't go to church; and apart from attending the occasional lecture at the Petro Jacyk Centre at the University of Toronto's Munk Centre, I don't adhere to any institution that could be described as Ukrainian Canadian. I don't make this admission with any sense of pride – in many ways I envy the friends of my university days who have gone on to join or actively work with organizations in the *hromada* or Ukrainian Canadian community; by temperament and circumstance, I have never been a joiner, and by marrying out of the community and raising my children with no focused awareness of their Ukrainian-ness, I have positioned myself as an outsider, although one who has at least a toehold inside the circle of belonging.

I could describe myself as belonging to the Ukrainian diaspora – but here, too, problems arise. When I last travelled in Ukraine, in 2005, whether I found myself in cities like Kyiv or Zhytomir, or in small villages on the river Zbruch, I found myself referred to as *Halychana*, or someone belonging to *Halychyna* – Galicia – the region from which so many Ukrainian diasporans have traditionally hailed. This geographical-cultural typecasting seemed a typical example of the tendency for insiders to disregard or fail to recognize differences of supreme importance to outsiders – *viz.* the general habit among Ukrainian villagers of referring to family visiting from Canada as *Amerikany*. Yet I feel my credentials as a *Halychana* to be non-existent, even false, for in the past decade I have become distanced from the influence and agency of the DPs, most of them born in western Ukraine – what was then Poland or Austria – and forced to work in German factories and farms during the Second World War. They had immigrated to North America in the late 1940s and early 1950s from the camps in which they'd been lodged by the Allied authorities, having resisted the Soviets' attempts to "repatriate" them to the USSR. The embrace by the DPs and their descendants of ethnic, even integral nationalism and linguistic purity can be seen as a predictable response to their experience of radical dislocation and dispossession. It was also an expression of their patriotic pride that saw western Ukraine assuming the role of Piedmont in the protracted struggle to establish an independent Ukraine.

Yet while I sympathize with the plight of the DPs, I reject attempts to impose onto contemporary Ukraine what I'd term the "diasporan romance" – a vision of a monocultural, monolingual nation of idyllic landscapes dotted with innocently bucolic villages, or cities in which only the Ukrainian language can be heard on the streets or in the home. As far as I can judge, the only progressive and ethical response to the question "What is Ukraine, and who is Ukrainian?" is one formulated in terms of civic rather than ethnic nationalism; one that recognizes the reality of independent Ukraine as a multicultural nation whose citizens, whether Jewish or Orthodox or Uniate or atheist; whether of Polish or Tatar or Armenian or Galician descent, and whether their first language be Ukrainian or Russian, struggle together to create a state that respects human rights, builds democratic institutions, combats corruption, and ensures the common good – economic, social, cultural. I do not believe these goals are incompatible with the survival and flourishing of the Ukrainian language; however difficult to achieve they may be, I find them vastly preferable to the mentality I saw expressed several years ago in a poster from Ukraine promoting the speaking of correct Ukrainian: a boot coming down on an insect representing a word whose origin was Polish or Russian or *surzhyk*.

I didn't always embrace the heterogeneous as opposed to homogeneous model of identity. As a child, I yearned to be 100 per cent *nashi* – "our own." My flawed identity declared itself in the very name by which I was christened: Janice Lynn Kulyk. Why, I lamented, hadn't my parents given me a name like Katrusia or Halyna instead of one starting with the letter J, for which there is no equivalent in Cyrillic, unless it is the award fusion of "d" and "zh." My grandmother called me Hania, the closest she could come to pronouncing Janice. And then, when I entered university, I affiliated myself differently: I studied English literature, I refused to belong to any Ukrainian clubs on campus, and I married, at the age of twenty, a man my family regarded as an "Englishman," though on his father's side his family had come to Canada in the 1790s. Yet calling myself Janice Keefer rather than Kulyk proved no solution to my problematic sense of self: shortly after I began to publish creative work in small literary journals I decided on an unhyphenated but up-front acknowledgment of my split self: I have published as Janice Kulyk Keefer ever since, though the name on my passport and health card remains Janice Keefer.

Betwixt and between: perhaps that's the most fruitful position for a writer to occupy, since the most interesting kinds of literature seem to stem from a conflicted rather than harmoniously composed temperament. Mavis Gallant once compared the writer to a *voyou*, which translates as "gangster" or "rascal" or at least someone who walks with one foot on and one off the curb. Certainly I am just such a curb-walker when it comes to my relation to the Ukrainian language, which is for me an affair of the heart – though not the valentine-simple version of *sertseh*. My first language, after all, was Ukrainian: lullabies and croonings, nonsense rhymes and clapping games, the background domestic noise of daily life. The two people whom I loved best as a child were my mother's parents, whose English was minimal: to my lasting regret, I was never able to speak Ukrainian with them in more than a childish way. They died many years ago, but to this day I grieve for the chance I never had to speak to them in the language in which they felt at home, in which they could be most themselves, expressing the thoughts and feelings that English locked up in them, perhaps in the same way that the hedge of thorns imprisoned Sleeping Beauty.

At My Grandparents' Graves

"Try to learn
a new word every day,
just one word – " you asked us,
so that we could speak together
in your native tongue.

Oh, we learned the rudiments:
names of food and dress,
serviceable words – language's
opposable thumbs. And since
you were fluent in the language of the heart,
what incentive was there for mastery? All those
declensions, conjugations that you knew
without learning: all those fences
my tongue could never jump.

Another kind of conversation, now:
the silences heart speaks to heart. What
was never, will never, be: to know you
as you knew yourselves:

heart's whole truth
unlocked from its separate chambers:
not just what becomes us
but what undoes us, too.

The stone-cut letters of your names;
shocked concision of a pair of dates.
The wind's language, as it nudges the yews
on either side of the granite.

Spirit blowing where it listeth
a pulse, made visible.
In Heaven, no giving in marriage,
and no divorce through words, just

radiance of touch,
all skin unscarred.
Our ears, our mouths
finally
       borderless.

    My lack of fluency in my grandparents' mother tongue must be an experience I share with many other children of immigrants in this country. Yet what has been for me a personal loss and lasting grief has also been a handicap vis-à-vis the creation of a meaningful sense of belonging to an entity, a community that in Ukrainian would be termed *ridniy* – my native, my own. Had I grown up "out west" in a city like Edmonton or Winnipeg or Saskatoon, where Canadians of Ukrainian descent have, for several generations, had a significant cultural presence, I would no doubt feel differently. My not knowing much Ukrainian would probably contribute to rather than detract from a sense of shared identity and certainly wouldn't be a source of shame or humiliation. I would probably have adopted a position similar to that of Canadian writer Clive Doucet vis-à-vis the French-speaking minority of the Maritimes. Of Acadian heritage through his father, Doucet is an anglophone whose work has been rejected by the Acadian elite and "cultural infrastructure" – his books are not stocked in the bookstores of Acadie, where he is considered an English Canadian writer, *tout court*. Yet in *Notes from Exile* Doucet makes a convincing case for extralinguistic ways of belonging to an *ethnos* through knowledge of history and cultural forms other than those transmitted through language and, especially, through an awareness of the ways in which a group who were once implacably "foreign" to Canada not only become Canadian, but alter and enrich the conventional idea of what Canadian-ness comprises.[2]

    But I am not a prairie "Uke": I grew up in Toronto, the child of immigrants who arrived in Canada just before the First and the Second World Wars from a place that was described as belonging to the Austro-Hungarian empire on my father's family's passports and to Poland on my mother's. My older sister's first spoken language was Ukrainian until she went to kindergarten: because of the menace of McCarthyism my parents decided to stop speaking Ukrainian in the home, with the result that my sister lost her first language and I never acquired it in any "natural" way. By the time I was old enough to attend Saturday Ukrainian school, by which time my parents' fears about drawing attention to their dangerous "otherness" had passed, English had become my mother tongue – Ukrainian had become a foreign language in which I might be able to ask for the butter at the dinner table, but whose grammar was an unfathomable mystery. Unlike friends who had grown up speaking Ukrainian with grandparents who lived in the home, or who were the children of DPs for whom fluency at a sophisticated level of Ukrainian was a *sine qua non* of existence, I was as good as mute: when I opened my mouth to try and speak Ukrainian, it was as though all the water in the world were rushing in, and all I could do was drown. I quickly learned the Cyrillic alphabet at Saturday school or *ridna shkola*; what fazed me was how words kept shifting and masking themselves – *dyeem* and *doma* both were the word for "home"; one tear was *slioza* but to be tearful was *povney sleez*.

My teachers at *ridna shkola* – most of them DPs – assumed that having been born to Ukrainian parents, I should have sucked in the language with my mother's milk: they must have believed it was perverse, spoiled stubbornness that kept me from communicating with them. Ditto my counsellors at summer camp, including the sadistic Marika, who regularly made me a linguistic laughingstock in front of my peers. When, at sixteen, I was sent to St Andrew's College in Winnipeg for summer school, I learned that Ukrainian was an inflected language, like Latin, which I was learning at high school. Yet memorizing declensions and conjugations couldn't undo the shame and humiliation in which my *ridna shkola* experience had drenched me. I went to university to study French and German, which I had started learning in high school; when I switched into English literature in my second year, and embarked on graduate studies in England a few years later, I left Ukrainian behind, especially after the death of my beloved grandmother – the only person with whom I had continued to speak some kind of Ukrainian, and speak it without the crushing sense that the language was a minefield; that at any moment I would use a wrong case ending and be blown sky-high. And whereas when I spoke French or German, I accepted the fact that I would make numerous errors which would either be corrected by my interlocutors, or smilingly tolerated, I was irrationally afraid of blundering when I spoke Ukrainian, as if anything short of perfect mastery of the language was the one unforgivable sin against the Holy Ghost.

All of this was an ironic inversion of my mother's family's experience on arriving in depression-era Toronto in 1936, unable to speak a word of English, yet expected to "make a go of it" in a society to which the concept of offering immigrants lessons in the dominant language was as foreign as those immigrants themselves. My mother, aged fourteen, was put in a kindergarten class by the principal of Charles G. Fraser school; my aunt, twelve, crawled under her desk when her teachers addressed her in English. Somehow, they learned – from watching Charlie Chaplin at the movies and listening to Lux Radio Theatre, and persevering in school, despite the mockery and terror they first experienced. For their parents, however, who spoke Polish as well as Ukrainian, all but the most elementary English remained *terra incognita*.

Slovar/Word Book

Thin, narrow, brown-red
of dried blood, fitting
the kind of narrow pockets no longer sewn:
bound in that oil cloth that simulates leather,

Flyleaf pencilled-in in Polish, with 3345678910
written the European way: slashed sevens;
ones tugging their forelocks. Who is Wasyl,
who Antsyl? Not even a family relic,
but a loan, never returned, except in this
imperfect, roundabout way –

passed down by my aunt while clearing out
her basement, so that her children
(none of whom speak Ukrainian)
won't have to deal with these
souvenirs of dislocation.

*

Embossed on the cover, a haloed
lion, and an angel with two crossed swords

30   Janice Kulyk Keefer

A Pocket-Dictionary
of the
English and Ukrainian
LANGUAGES

giving the pronunciation of English
words in Ukrainian characters and
Ukrainian sounds.

Published by
Ruthenian Booksellers and Publishers
Limited.
848–850 Main Street – Winnipeg Canada

*

Asiatic
Oh!
Act
Midwife

Artemis
artery
artillery

Abirration
Bawdy
Contumely.

Who made up this list?
Prairie sadists? Drunken lexicographers? Poets
seeking revenge on people who'd choose
that pair of boots over Shakespeare?

*

Komensment off samer
Vachmen
Clovdeeng.

My grandparents, needing the words for
soap, bus (though they usually walked
to save the fare – the price of a loaf of bread)

Words with penciled stars beside them:

room, rent and,
God forbid, doctor.

Armed not with a Bible but a pocket dictionary
to stop bullets of words. A charm against the easy
power of those needing no phonetic guide
to the language spoken by cops
and courts, anyone
with the power to send them back

to that country already old,
impossible: war, hunger
graves: the things themselves, and not
just words.

*

More than thirty years after I had stopped trying to speak Ukrainian, I was awarded a research grant to travel to post–Orange Revolution Ukraine. I had written a novel and a family memoir dealing with Ukrainian-ness – my own and that of imagined others – and I had read books on Ukrainian history, but I had never sat down to wrestle once more with Podvesko's Ukrainian dictionary and my old Slavyutych Grammar book (translate into Ukrainian: In the forest grow tall, green trees. I see the tall, green tree. Birds are on the tall tree. The birds have fine nests. The birds have nests on the tall trees. Above the tall trees, the birds fly and sing.) I decided the time had come to exorcise the language demons trapped in my brain and tongue: I enrolled in an intermediate-level language course at the University of Toronto's Slavic Studies Department. For the next three months I was consumed by the effort of learning enough of the language to be able to speak and read at the level of a reasonably educated adult. I don't think I have ever worked so hard, or set myself a more Herculean, possibly Sisyphean task.

Rushing to class against rush-hour traffic in the grey dusk of winter, through a world that seemed utterly unaware of and uninterested in the Ukrainian language, I experienced a salutory change of perspective: here I was, a university prof, just one among a group of students – and the worst student of the bunch, at that. For three hours each week I'd sit in a windowless cinderblock classroom, stale and stuffy, as though the air, by evening, were crammed with the words and sighs and yawns of every student who had sat there during the day. The students – all but me in their early twenties – had all grown up in Ukrainian. They'd learned it from *babusia*, or they'd gone to a bilingual English–Ukrainian school, or had attended pedagogically effective heritage language classes. At any rate they were comfortable conversing in Ukrainian in an everyday, conversational way, with accents that varied from perfect to competent – whereas I was fearful, paralysed with embarrassment, *déclassée*.

The students would meet some fifteen minutes before class, assembling on the sofas and chairs in the lounge, frantically reviewing for tests or collaborating on the homework they should have done days earlier. The students were mostly young women, and ranged from a red-headed immigrant from Poland who spoke with the most ravishing accent – though she complained that in Poland Ukrainians tend to hide their mother tongue and are reduced to speaking a dialect – to a Canadian-born student who wished she were learning the language from scratch, so there'd be no interference with what she'd learned "wrong" from her family. But all of them had grown up in a world in which an independent Ukraine actually existed; none of them had been raised to carry the torch for a language and culture and imagined community that, as the national anthem expresses it, is not dead yet (but by corollary is on its very last legs ...).

Our professor was young, dapper, and possessed of a ready sense of humour. A respected scholar, he was a superb pedagogue as well, and not just because he would enliven a class in the uses of the dative case by tossing a plush toy pig about, teaching us the expression "slip a pig to someone," that is, play a trick on them. The language we were learning in our evening class was Ukrainian as spoken in the age of computers and mobile phones and satellite television. From Xeroxes of want ads and other advertising, of magazine articles and contemporary short fiction, we were given access to Ukrainian slang and idioms that those in "the Community" with an investment in a fossilized, idealized culture would no doubt frown upon. One of the students, on encountering a story in which a prostitute figured, became uncomfortable: "We didn't learn things like this in Ukrainian school," she protested. The professor took the objection in his stride. Ukrainian-born and raised, though he got his doctorate from Harvard, he was as committed to teaching Ukrainian as a living language as he was optimistic about the future of Ukraine. When he spoke to me of the publishing scene in Kyiv, and how well Ukrainian-language publishers – especially of children's books – were doing, it seemed a staunch corrective to my anxiety that the Ukrainian-language publishing industry would be closing down as quickly and completely as the Ukrainian-language film industry had done.

Once and again, I found myself betwixt and between – in this case, between the group of carefree, hang-up-less students and the confident professor; between my focused desire to "learn the language once and for all" and my inability to make the leap into fluency. By the end of the course, I felt like a lover who has been repeatedly slighted, laughed at, shunned – given the pumpkin! (In village life and lore, a girl who is being courted by a suitor she doesn't relish will leave a pumpkin outside the front door as the equivalent of a Dear John letter.) The intricacies of Slavic tongues can be cruel for non-native speakers. For example, in Ukrainian there is no simple equivalent for "come and go," *venir et aller, kommen und gehen*. Using verbs of motion can be like playing three-dimensional chess, since you have to decide, before a sound escapes your mouth, whether you're going in one direction, or to a variety of places; whether you're setting out on foot or in a vehicle. Numbers are treacherous: the genitive case must be used for all numbers between four and twenty-one, at least, I think that's the rule. *Try* (three) *khloptsi* (boys) but *chotyri* (four) *khloptsiv*. There are three genders, as in German, but an extra three cases. Add to that a penchant for the polysyllabic, so that "pleased to meet you" becomes pree-YEM-no ZVA-my poz-nai-OM-yt-is-ya. . . .

Ars Grammatica

represented, allegorically, by the figure
of a chastely beautiful woman watering
a row of flowerpots figuring
the strict-stemmed rules of grammar.

Start with the name, Ukraine:
Latin alphabet dictates U-kraine
as in U-turn or U-bend. Sometimes
pronounced Oo-ker-ain
by the same kind of people who say
nuke-yu-lur.

Oo-kra-yee-na.
Noun, feminine: that "a'
extending past the final consonant.
Sound of a sigh, pleasure or regret,
or a compound of both –

Yet, even with something simple as a name,
complications crash. Oo-kra-yee-na
becomes Oo-krayeenu, Ookrayeeni, Ookrayeenoyu, depending on
use: subject, object (direct or indirect)
or instrumental case. The final 'a" of *UkraYEEna*
indicates the nominative, that virginal
state of being as one is,

oneself, uncolonized.
Certainly being, perhaps doing,
but absolutely not
being done to.

To say Ukraine in any alphabet but Cyrillic,
is to speak in a condition not just
of transliteration, but also
of translation, which is another word for error,
as in wandering, *errare*. Not just words,
but the very letters from which words are stitched,
pure symbols as those letters be, refuse to pose, connect
like petals at their base, becoming flower. Instead,
they sting, not prettily, not
the nips that puzzle Cranach's cupid,
holding up the plundered honey comb,
but bites that rasp and scorch,
swelling the skin on which they're inked:
YKPAIHA, yik-pay-ha?

Start with a word; stopped
by a word – barbed wire? Or
a stile, part of a fence that keeps you out,
but also a way up
and over, a thing
making movement possible, however
rough and ready, however up
and down.

There were times when, sweating over my grammar books and exercises, I passionately hated Ukrainian – wished it at the bottom of the sea or the ends of the earth, exulting in the thrill of transgression: harbouring animosity to *mova ridna*, the sacred chalice in which Ukrainianness is supposed to reside! Why not simply walk away from it forever, or else concede defeat? When I posed this question to myself as a child and adolescent, the answer I knew my teachers would give me brooked no debate. Roughly summarized, it was this: Ukrainians in the diaspora have the sacred task of keeping the language alive by speaking it with their children and insisting on its proper use in their community and its organizations. The Ukrainian language has been persecuted, harassed, demeaned, penalized, and outlawed by Ukraine's long chain of occupiers and colonizers, up to and including the Russifying Communists. If it dies, its blood will be on your hands – and in your mouth!

Later, I did my own research on the persecution of the Ukrainian language. I discovered, among other things, that thanks to the Ems Ukaz of 1876, whereby Tsar Alexander II prohibited the use of the Ukrainian language for all purposes of education, entertainment, publication, and emergency information, not only were Ukrainian-language plays banned from theatres in Ukraine, but publicly posted warnings about cholera epidemics in towns and villages could only be printed in Russian, whether the inhabitants understood that language or not. There were more subtle ways of diminishing the expressive possibilities and denying the very validity of the Ukrainian language – demoting it to the status of mere "Little Russian" dialect or delimiting its literary uses to burlesque and broad satire. Before the Ems Ukaz, assiduous censorship with draconian repercussions ensured that in eastern or Russian-ruled Ukraine, Shevchenko apart, Ukrainian writers of genius wrote and published in Russian. And in western Ukraine, which experienced a far milder form of autocracy via the Hapsburg Empire, Ukrainians for all their freedom to publish were denied access to university education in their mother tongue. In Soviet Ukraine, the flowering of Ukrainian culture in the 1920s, which produced literary works and experimental theatre of an exceptional quality, was cut brutally short by the terror of the 1930s. One of Ukraine's finest modern poets, Vasyl' Stus, died in 1985 in a gulag where he had spent twenty-three years for the crime of writing in Ukrainian, of being a vocal Ukrainian dissident.[3] Imprisonment of this horrific kind was the lot of many Ukrainian writers and artists of the 1960s. In today's independent Ukraine, the flourishing – even the survival – of the Ukrainian language is not a given: Russian speakers predominate on the street, in the shops, and most egregiously on television and radio and in the cinema. Western entertainment is wholly mediated through the Russian language. And many of the people of Ukraine feel most at home neither in Russian nor in Ukrainian but in a mixture of these languages, *surzhyk*, a hybrid that is usually derided and treated with contempt.

It is a situation that should be countered by the coming of age of a generation of Ukrainians who will, for the first time in the country's history, have accomplished all their schooling, from elementary through secondary to university and postgraduate work, in Ukrainian. These students, though they will have a casual acquaintance with Russian, will not have studied it; Ukrainian will be their language of preference for all spoken and written discourse at a civic and professional level, or so the theory goes. Yet with Ukraine's economy as fragile as it is, and the country's politics as fraught as they are, the "normalization" of Ukrainian – as opposed to its constitutional protection as the sole state language – will be difficult, though not impossible to accomplish. Western popular culture is mediated through the Russian language, and the prestige of Ukrainian outside the country is precarious. To take one example, while a novel like *Death and the Penguin*, written in Russian by Kyivan Andrey Kurkov, is easily available in English translation, works of fiction by Kurkov's equally talented Ukrainian-language contemporaries are not. Poet and novelist Oksana Zabushko – often referred to in Ukraine as that country's Margaret Atwood – has bemoaned the low profile of the Ukrainian arts in Europe, as well as her government's utter lack of interest in promoting an awareness of the sophisticated forms of Ukrainian culture in general. Given how many Americans assume that Atwood is American born and bred, it could be argued that in the cultural realm, Russian is to Ukrainian what American is to Canadian.

*

"And why are you learning Ukrainian?" asked X.
What I heard was this: "Why are you bothering to learn Ukrainian?"
I answered with a question: "If I had said I was learning Russian, would you have asked why?"
"Hmmm," X mutters. "Probably not."

*

It was difficult enough, during the period when I was taking that evening Ukrainian class, to memorize vocabulary and try to make everyday expressions roll off my tongue. But I also had to deal with the incomprehension of friends and colleagues who simply couldn't fathom why I would devote time and energy to learning this, of all languages. It was a version of the cautions expressed by some friends of the family when my younger brother decided, in the 1970s, that he was going to put his energies into learning how to speak, read, and write Ukrainian, instead of doing make-up classes in maths and sciences. "But why Ukrainian? It's a dying language. Learn Russian if you must learn a Slavic tongue – it's a world language, it's spoken by powerful people – it will be of some use to you at least."

And here is the crux of one matter: Russian is one of the major languages of the world, while Ukrainian is, to use François Paré's term, an exiguous one.[4] Russian is the language of Bulgakov and Chekhov and Babel, Pushkin, Tsvetayeva, and Mandelstam, never mind Tolstoy and Dostoevsky. Who wouldn't long to be able to read these giants in the original? The Ukrainian equivalents of these writers, however, are utterly unknown to most educated people outside the culture; others would assert that there simply are no Ukrainian equivalents, that Ukrainian is merely a dialect of Russian anyway – why else did the Ukrainian Hohol, better known to the world as Gogol, write in Russian? And as for Shevchenko, Ukraine's national poet, the English translations of his work with which I'm familiar are so appalling that it's almost better that they not be known. But let's put matters of literary value, the aesthetics of translation, and the linguistic and cultural fate of brutally colonized countries aside for the moment. Why, I might have asked X, does anyone learn another language, assuming that they can "get by" in their own? Especially if the latter is the English language, the *lingua franca* of the twenty-first century (though Mandarin may just replace it in the twenty-second). Ukrainians are learning English as eagerly, now, as anyone else, as I discovered when visiting Kyiv. So why would anyone outside the country try – bother – to learn Ukrainian?

I could say that you learn another language for the same reason that you travel to another country: to try and climb outside of your own skin, to grow a different set of ears and eyes. To undergo that voluntary displacement that permits learning to occur. For sensuous reasons – for the delight of unaccustomed and rewarding sounds on your tongue, in your mouth – a linguistic version of gastronomy. And arguing from my own case, I could point to the curious joy of reclamation: after a childhood spent memorizing what seemed like yards of opaque patriotic verse, learning dozens of folk songs – or the phonetic approximations of their incomprehensible lyrics – attending church services for which I provided my own translations, turning the refrain *hospodi pomilui*, for example, into "sunny vanilla," a celestial flavour of ice cream – I have been able, however belatedly, to connect words and meanings. It was largely for this – the delight of delayed learning, the perceptual thrill of holding what had formerly been a dark piece of glass to the light and seeing it suddenly turn transparent – that I had set myself to learn Ukrainian. I had, long before this, discovered that *hospodi pomilui* meant "lord have mercy." But the word *chudo*, which I'd first heard as a child in a Christmas carol – only a lifetime later did I discover that it meant "wonder" or "marvel."

And there have been rewards far more precious. Language is the cradle of memory; words, as individual as images, have the power to restore to us what has seemed to have perished. Sifting through grammar texts and dictionaries, trying to recapture a language I never really knew, I chanced upon the word *hoydaty*, to swing. I was seized by a memory in the flesh as well as the mind: being a small child, swung in my grandfather's arms, as he chanted *hoy-day, hoy-dah*. The remembering was so real, brought me so close inside the skin and bones of that two- or even one-year-old: the sound of that word, the feel of the arms that swung me ...

*

In spite of the excellence of my professor, I failed to learn to speak Ukrainian with ease and accuracy and anything approaching *sprezzatura*. I have accepted the fact of my radical speech impediment, as far as the mastery of my parents' mother tongue is concerned. I have not, however, given up on Ukrainian. The research project in which I'm currently engaged involves me in making rough – very rough – translations of certain Ukrainian-language texts into English. I could, if I had resources enough, hire someone to do the translating, but I find myself more and more engrossed with a task that, though onerous, is also profoundly satisfying. I will have to seek out the help of a native speaker to check any translations that I intend to put into print, but for now, I am finding my feet and even beginning, if not to dance, then to skip occasionally, as I make my way through page after page of Cyrillic. Perhaps my current state of insouciance vis-à-vis Ukrainian is the freedom of age – not caring so much, anymore, what people will say or think of what I do or leave undone. And perhaps I have found, at last, a community in which I can feel at home, a community composed not of any one ethnic or linguistic group, but of all those who are stranded between languages, or struggling to make their peace with the demands of different cultures. And so, I will end with a poem that has emerged out of my recognizing what a common experience it is, here and now, to be *ni te, ni se*: betwixt and between.

Language Lessons

At the Y, I share the sauna
with half a dozen Latinas, all
speaking runaway Spanish, some
of which I understand: *problema, hombres,
no tengo bastante dinero.*

On the streetcar going home,
a woman and her small son:
her stream of Spanish – his fists
in his ears. *Speak English, Mommy,
I don't understand.*

(Compared to *Mamacita*
it sounds odd, even ugly –
the whine, the aggravated shove
of *Mommy*.)

She keeps on,
patient, insistent;
he keeps chanting
in perfect North American:
Speak English.

As they make
for the exit, he stops,
stoops, shows
the glove she's dropped:

As if to prove himself right;
as if in any other language
he wouldn't have been able
to find and offer it –

She holds out her hand;
he puts the glove in it.
Both of them
without a word.

NOTES

1 See Ledohowski, "Ukrainian Canadian Poet Pedagogues."
2 Doucet, *Notes from Exile*.
3 He is the Ukrainian "doomed bridegroom" in Myrna Kostash's book of that same name, and she writes of him again, here, in this book, situating him alongside Wandering Spirit and St Demetrius.
4 Paré, *Exiguity*, 26.

2 Eight Things

ELIZABETH BACHINSKY

People tell me that Vera Lysenko was the first Ukrainian Canadian to write in English; her 1947 *Men in Sheepskin Coats* received vitriolic reviews in part because of rampant anticommunist sentiment.[1] God forbid that she get funding from an organization with so-called commie tendencies. McCarthyism wasn't just an American phenomenon, was it?

But I digress.

I am thinking about writing. Ukrainian Canadian writing, but the kind written in English.

Before Lysenko, there was a Bachinsky, well, actually a Bychinsky (sometimes credited as Buchinsky), and you'll forgive me for seeing me in her and her in me – an "a" for a "y" after all is such an easy swap, a "u" even easier. Anna Bychinsky wrote two short stories for *Maclean's* magazine back in the 1920s.[2] Why didn't I learn that in school? Did she know my Michael?[3] Was he a long-lost relation locked behind Canadian barbed wire while she sat safely in the United States behind a desk scribbling her stories that would appear after the war? Only after the war. Did they know each other? Were they related back in the "Old Country"? Did their mothers send letters one to the other worrying about their prodigal children overseas, never to come home? Did they write as sisters, as cousins?

I write to my sister.

I am telling you this because my sister is my muse. When she lived as an art student in Montreal, I wrote a long poem to express the profound sadness I felt at her living there and my living without her in Vancouver. And when I began my research for my third collection of poetry *God of Missed Connections* – which I like to say is my self-education in the history of my ancestors – it was towards my sister that my voice could not help but reach.

When I write to my sister, I also write to the thousands of third-generation Ukrainian Canadians with whom we share ancestry. And I also write to myself.

I was born at Regina General Hospital in 1976, the first daughter of Peter and Catherine Bachinsky (née Gnuis), who first met in 1968 at a Ukrainian dance camp in Husavik, Manitoba, when they were teenagers. My parents were talented dancers who had grown up immersed in a non-religious Ukrainian Canadian community on the prairies. My dad was from Winnipeg, my mom from Regina. The story of how my parents met is legend in our family of four, especially because not long after I was born, we started to travel. My dad was in the Air Force so, like many military families, we moved from town to town, base to base, until, finally, my father left the military to work for a private helicopter company in Prince George, in north-central BC. I hear that in 2011 there is a somewhat large Ukrainian Canadian community in Prince George, but when we were living there in the 1980s, this did not appear to be the case. My sister and I attended public schools, sang in the community choir, and attended an Anglican Church on Sundays. We did not have any extended family in Prince George. The only time we saw our grandparents, aunts, uncles, and cousins was at Christmas, when either we drove to the prairies for a visit or they came to us. I would not say that my sister and I knew very much about what it meant to be a part of a Ukrainian Canadian community.

Here are the eight things that we knew:

1. Our entire extended family lived in Saskatchewan, Manitoba, and Ontario.
2. Our parents had once been Ukrainian dancers.
3. How to pinch perogies.
4. Cabbage rolls taste good. Mom makes them every Christmas.
5. We get Christmas twice: once in December for "regular Christmas" and then again in January for Ukrainian Christmas, which is marked by a phone call to Baba in Winnipeg and Granny in Regina.
6. During Multicultural Days at elementary school, we wear traditional Ukrainian dance costumes with wide red skirts and white blouses decorated with embroidery.
7. Mom's Granny Minnie came from Belfast, Ireland.
8. Everybody else in our family came from Ukraine.

This was about the extent of our education in our ancestry for a very long time: cabbage rolls taste good; we get Christmas twice. It is not that we weren't interested in stories about Ukraine. It is that there weren't any ... and, besides, our Ukrainian-ness was a lot like the colour of our skin and our eyes. We were as Ukrainian as our skin was white and our eyes were brown. You could never say to us, your skin is not white. Your eyes are not brown. It was, and they were. If someone asked us where we were from, we said Canada. When pressed, Ukraine.

As we got older, we learned a few more things: that our father did not speak English until he was four years old – until then, having been raised by his grandparents in Winnipeg, he spoke only Ukrainian – and we were lucky to have an amateur historian in our aunt who sent pictures of our ancestors at Christmas, images of our great-grandfather Michael Bachinsky in an Austrian military uniform in the "Old Country" and our grandfather Peter Bachinsky (for whom our father is named) in his Canadian military uniform during the Second World War. And sometimes our mother would tell us what it was like to dance with the Poltava Dancers in Regina and that Dad had been headhunted by the Royal Winnipeg Ballet, but declined the invitation. But mom didn't tell these stories very often, and, as is often the case with beginning students, since we didn't know much, we didn't know what to ask.

In 2005, I got a phone call from my friend Trish Kelly (née Chornyj), with whom I planned to study the Ukrainian language in Vancouver.

"So, how are things going in the homeland?" she asked.

"Prince George?" I said.

"No. the Old Country," she replied.

I was caught off guard. I didn't have an answer for her because I didn't know. The "Old Country"? Ukraine? What's happening in *Ukraine*?[4] I often tell this story when people ask me why I wrote *God of Missed Connections*, and this is why: what I realized the moment Trish called me was that I had taken my ancestry for granted. Perogies and cabbage rolls and the Royal Winnipeg Ballet had always been enough for me, until then. Now I was curious. Now I felt like a fool. How could I continue to claim a heritage without having any sense of the history?

For the next several years I made it my business to answer Trish's question. Not only for myself, but also for my sister, who also had many unanswered questions. This was the beginning of the problem of how to research a community with whom I identified but who I did not "know."

Here are eight problems to knowing:

1. *I'm Ukrainian, but I don't "feel" Ukrainian.*
2. *I don't speak or write Ukrainian.*
3. *What do you mean I'm not white? What does it mean to be an ethnic Ukrainian?*
4. *Where are all the books?*
5. *Where is all the art and media by third- and fourth-generation Ukrainian Canadians?*
6. *Stereotypes in popular culture keep us from really knowing anything.*
7. *Why didn't I know about the* Holodomor *and the internment of Ukrainian Canadians during the First World War?*[5]
8. *What do I do about all this?*

The Wax Ceremony[6]

>And the soothsayer prophesied.
>Charming the evil eye,
>For three coins,
>Pouring destiny and fortune from the wax.
>– Taras Shevchenko

2005. A woman, twenty-nine. Dark hair pulled back into a ponytail. Ankles crossed beneath her desk. She sits in a rented room before a small white laptop computer. She types,

1911. Michael Bazynski [sic] sits, seasick, in the hold of a ship that sailed from Odessa. Though he believes he will be welcomed in his new country, he will not be surprised to learn that he is mistaken. He won't have enough money to get home.

Come out of hiding, baba, she says. Teach me to pour the wax.

What does she see from her window? Apartment buildings. Hastings Street. She takes a book from her desk and reads,

> A little dose of them may even in variation, do good, like a minute dose of poison in medicine ... I am not saying we should absolutely shut out and debar the European foreigner as we should and do the Oriental. But we should in no way facilitate his coming.
> – Stephen Leacock, 1930.

> *You are all of this Pain and Suffering.*
> *Prickly and sore,*
> *I enjoin and summon you,*
> *From the head, from under the head.*
> *From the crown of the head,*
> *From under the crown of the head,*

On some construction sites, she writes, there is a big machine that construction workers use to separate different-sized stones. When I was a kid, I played with a small plastic version of this same machine. Tip the toy in one direction and all the different-sized marbles fall into a reservoir. Tip it in the other direction and only the smallest marbles make it through. Many get sifted out. A radio has switched on in a distant room. It whispers the news, traffic patterns, advertisements for hamburgers. The radio competes with Lars von Trier's *The Five Obstructions* playing on the DVD player in the living room. Both sounds are in the background. This page is the foreground.

1911. Paris, France. Stephen Leacock sips eau do vie. At 27 Rue de Fleurus, Gertrude makes love to Alice. Tomorrow the women would like to buy paintings. "Remember," Gertrude says. "We never hid. We moved to Paris."

"Yes, Love," says Alice. "We did that."

1914. Winnipeg, Canada: Michael Baczynski boards a train bound for Banff, Alberta, where there is a labour camp in the Rockies. He will lie there six years.

How does the girl work? Like this.

Soldiers put Michael on a train bound for a work camp in the Rockies with sixteen other young men. Some, Michael knew from AUUC meetings at the Labour Temple in Winnipeg, others he did not. West of Calgary, he saw his first mountains. Dizzying, rising black-green from roiling lapis-coloured water. The forests so dense it was impossible to discern the land beneath them. And then the land finally did appear, a white swath of ice curing upward like the bottom of a terrible basin.

From the eyes, from under the eyes,
From the nose, from under the nose,
From the mouth, from under the mouth,

The prisoners cut two-by-two-foot blocks of ice from the Bow River and loaded them, dripping, onto low flat wagons. Half a million blocks in all – and all the while, that strange pale green Bow water sluiced below the surface of the ice. That same water the men watched funnel past the quarries all summer as they cut stone from Tunnel Mountain for the hotel across the valley. Days heaped upon them.

Monday, January 29, 1917.

Fine, cloudy, very cold – some snow. Temperature, –11° Max. and –20° Min. No prisoners of war out on park work a.m. or p.m. – too cold.

Tuesday, January 30, 1917.

Fine, cloudy, very, very cold. Temperature, –30° Max. and –36° Min. No prisoners of war out on park work due to extreme cold weather in a.m.

Wednesday, January 31.

Fine, cloudy, extremely cold. Temperature –25° Max. and –43° Min. No prisoners of war out on park work in a.m. In p.m. 20 prisoners of war escorted by 25 troops worked at toboggan slide from 2 p.m. to 4:30 p.m. Extremely cold with raw east wind.

As the morning progresses, the girl becomes concerned with breathing, eating, fucking, shitting. What is she thinking about? Downstairs, her Chinese-speaking neighbours are smoking. So, there is a downstairs. She can smell the neighbours' smoke. Their smoke makes her aware of them, and a little annoyed. When it is time to use the kitchen, she is careful not to run the microwave and the kettle at the same time for fear of tripping the breaker. If she trips the breaker, she will have to go downstairs and ask the neighbours to flip it. They may not understand her. She types,

I have some money.

I have my own money?

> *From the neck, from under the neck,*
> *From the ears, from the hearing,*
> *From the nape, from under the nape,*

1933. Eastern Ukraine. A Party official writes,

I saw people dying in solitude by slow degree, dying hideously without the excuse of sacrifice for a cause. They had been trapped and left to starve, each in his home, by a political decision made in a far-off capital around conference and banquet tables.

1934. Alberta. A farmer clears land that won't yield for fifteen years. A police officer leans nearby, watches, gnaws the end of a carrot he pulled from a garden at the side of the house. What about deportation, he says. Don't you care about being made to leave?

You see how my kids are dressed, the farmer replies. You see what furniture we have, what food we eat. Do you think it is possible for life to be any worse?

No, says the policeman.

2007. British Columbia.
She eats.

1932–1933. Holodomor.

She can't begin to write
about this.

How to repress a memory

1: The event must be proven to be true.

2: The persons to whom the event occurred must not speak
of the event for many years.

Write one true thing, then another.

>
> *From the shoulders, from under the shoulders,*
> *From the chest, from under the chest*
> *From the viscera, from under the viscera,*

"These Are Your Parks," said the park brochure. "Come and Enjoy Them."

In the Danish film, Jørgen Leth's perfect woman speaks perfect French, is blonde-haired and blue-eyed smokes, suicidally, inside an expensive-looking car. In the film, she uses a bidet.

She can't begin to write. What then?

She types,

O. I am making love. My husband's hands are on either side of my body. He lies behind me on our bed and enters me. He holds his cock still inside me. He reaches around and holds my breasts in either hand. I twist so that my back is flat on the bed, while my hips remain turned. In this position, my husband can kiss my breasts while still fucking me from behind. Now, his mouth is very close to my ear. He whispers to me, kisses my neck, my ears, my eyes. In this position, I am able to close my legs tightly around him. The sound of my husband's voice is effective. Now, it is effective. He has asked me if I might come. I do.

Rich folks have complicated ways of dealing with their shit. Three-ply toilet paper. Bidets. All those rich assholes perched over the cleanest porcelain.

> *From the guts, from under the guts,*
> *From seventy joints*
> *From the lower back, from under the lower back,*

Memory Fact Parenthesis

The actual

What they called their policies

What their policies were

Another thing I am interested in is

I wonder why

A question I have is

Why must I write about my lovemaking?

So that I might remember it.

> As for the Galicians I have not met a single person in the whole of the Northwest who is sympathetic towards them. They are from the point of view of civilization, ten times lower than the Indians.
> – Father Morin, *Alberta Tribune*, 4 February 1899

Im(migrant).

No. Not the present tense.

My name. Here,

………………………………………………………………..

From the thighs, from under the thighs,
From the knees, from under the knees
From the calves, from under the calves,

Thursday, February 1, 1917.

Fine, cloudy, extremely cold – worst yet but signs of changing. Temperature –3° Max. and –50° Min. No prisoners of war out on park work in a.m. except 24 for Ice Place and 40 for toboggan slide who left camp at 10:40 a.m. In p.m. temperature moderated and gangs were out at Recreation Park, Cave and Basin Rd.

Saturday, February 3, 1917.

Early a.m. – very mild – dull, cloudy at 9 a.m. 24° above, at 11 a.m. 14° below. Started snowing from east at 10:30 a.m.

154 prisoners of war out on park work. Lieutenant Davis left for noon on duty to Calgary. No work by prisoners of war in p.m. Tickets were given out to prisoners of war in p.m. about 20 refused to sign payroll.

alone. alone. alone.

Michael took a knife and carved a hole in his gut, but he didn't die. He crawled beneath his bunk and slit his neck. *These men will end us. The barracks, the wire, the white mountains. All dead. All dead.*

These are your Vermilion Lakes, Michael. Open them. And, oh yes, his blood drained from him in the dark. When soldiers found him drowning, not

one said, *Oh, but he is dead, he is dead.*

> *From the ankles, from under the ankles*
> *From the middle of the feet, from under the middle of the feet,*
> *From the toes, from under the toes,*

Internment camps, 1914–1920

Halifax
Quebec
Montreal
Toronto
Kingston
Petewawa
Spirit Lake
Kapuskasing
Brandon
Lethbridge
Vernon
Nanaimo
Port Arthur
Amherst

Among the interned:

Ukrainians (Ruthenians, Galicians)
Poles
Germans
Hungarians
Romanians
conscientious objectors
Some women
Some children
Mostly men

She types,

In my family, we don't speak of family.
And we don't speak of the past.

What is there to know? I'm not afraid to ask.

> Canadians were afraid not only that this imported proletariat could not be assimilated, but also that it would drag down Western society and destroy the British character of the country.
> – Jaroslav Petryshyn, 1985

> *From the soles, from under the soles.*
> *Go there beyond the range of dogs' barking,*
> *Beyond cocks' crowing, where people do not go,*
> *Where church services are not conducted!*
> *I give you a hen with chicks, a cat with kittens*
> *A sow with piglets, a duck with ducklings, a goose*
> *with goslings.*

The morning is finished.

Bars of light slant through the blinds.

She types,

Look up: Proleteriat

> *Go away, take them with you, and carry them with you*
> *To the blue seas, to deep streams*
> *There you will sift through sand, bathe in water,*
> *Wrap yourself in a leaf!*
> *Swing on a branch.*

NOTES

1 Kirkconnell, Review of *Yellow Boots*.
2 Bychinsky, "The Dowry"; Bychinsky, "Zonia's Revolt" (inaccurately attributed to A. Kuryla Buchinski).
3 Michael Bachinsky was my great-grandfather; there is another Michael Bazynski who was interned in Canada during the First World War as an enemy alien. In my poetry I blend these identities in my poetic ruminations.
4 Here, of course, I refer to the Orange Revolution that saw thousands of Ukrainian protesters take to the streets and camp out in tents to call for a new election.
5 The *Holodomor* was the Ukrainian genocide-by-famine of 1932–3 during which millions of Ukrainians starved to death. During the First World War, Canada's first national internment operation saw thousands of Canadians of Eastern European descent (including Ukrainians) interned as "enemy aliens." In 2008 the Canadian government recognized this internment and established a $10 million endowment fund for educational and commemorative activities to raise awareness of this internment.
6 Bachinsky, "The Wax Ceremony," in *God of Missed Connections*, www.nightwoodeditions.com. Reprinted with permission. "The Wax Ceremony" draws on a number of print and online research materials. Those interested in a complete bibliography may contact the author through Nightwood Editions. Texts of particular significance to "The Wax Ceremony" include Bohdan Kordan and Peter Melnycky's *In the Shadow of the Rockies*; Bill Waiser's *Park Prisoners*; Orest Martynowych's *Ukrainians in Canada*; Helen Potrebenko's *No Streets of Gold*; and the NFB film *Freedom Had a Price*.

3 Am I Ukrainian?

MARSHA FORCHUK SKRYPUCH

I was born in Canada. My parents were born in Canada. My mother's ancestors crossed the ocean before there was a Canada, from France and Ireland.

A century ago, my grandfather came here from Bykovyna when it was part of the Austro-Hungarian Empire, but Canada interned him as an enemy alien in the First World War,[1] and the prejudice he endured carried on to the next generation. My father had the Ukrainian beaten out of him at elementary school in Alberta. His teachers changed his name from Myroslav to Marshall (which is how I got the un-Ukrainian name of Marsha). Dad vowed that his own kids wouldn't suffer like he did, so he didn't teach us Ukrainian.

It is not the sense of being Ukrainian that resonates most deeply for me; it's the sense of not belonging. Whether it was as a child in the 1960s with divorced parents going to a Catholic school, or as a dyslexic in a system that promoted a single way of learning, I was always the outsider.

I yearned to connect with people like me – people who didn't quite fit in. Once I finally taught myself how to read at the age of nine, I devoured library books like *Oliver Twist, Little Women, Black Like Me, The Diary of Anne Frank*. At night, with flashlight in hand, I'd sneak out of bed and grab one of my mother's fat historicals from the shelf outside my room – novels by Daphne du Maurier, Taylor Caldwell, Irving Stone.

Literature became the world where I could connect.

Trudeau's policy of multiculturalism unfolded when I was in high school. My home town of Brantford initiated its own International Village festivities and this piqued my interest in my Ukrainian heritage.

But much as I liked making *pysanky* and eating *pyrohy*, I couldn't find stories about the Ukrainian experience. I know now that they existed, but in the 1970s in my town, they were not available. Once again, I felt like a bit of an outsider, so I immersed myself in novels about other Eastern Europeans – Poles, Jews, Russians.

In university, I wanted to take Ukrainian to fulfil my language requirement for my English degree. It wasn't available, so I took Russian instead. Ironically, taking Russian is what led me back to my Ukrainian roots.[2]

Most of the people in class were native Russian speakers, taking the credit to boost their grade averages. I didn't even know the alphabet, so had to make myself flashcards to practise on the bus ride to school each day, first just the letters, then the words, then the declensions. Amidst the Russians was one Ukrainian – Natalia. When she found out that I was of Ukrainian heritage, she took me under her wing. I helped her too – essay writing in English was not her forte – so it was an even swap. The following year, we became roommates. Meeting Natalia filled a gap in my life that I didn't know existed. She introduced me to Ukrainian culture and history and tutored me in the language. She took me to *zabavas* where I met my future husband.

As I learned more and more about being Ukrainian, I began to be confronted with a kind of shame attached to Ukrainian-ness. Blockbuster novels and television miniseries on the Holocaust flooded popular perceptions about the Second World War. And while this attention went a long way in shedding light on anti-Semitism, the simplified portrayal of events perpetuated other prejudices. As an example, Ukrainians were no longer seen as simple, friendly, unthreatening egg decorators and acrobatic dancers; now they were Nazi camp guards and killers.

Like my father before me, I became ashamed of my Ukrainian name.

But my father didn't have a Natalia to help him make sense of his identity and those feelings of shame. I did. Natalia told me that being a death camp guard and killer was shameful; being Ukrainian was not. More than that, she told me that there was more to the Ukrainian story of the Second World War. She told me of her mother, who had been taken as a slave by the Nazis, and of her father, who had been a Red Army soldier taken as a prisoner of war by the Nazis. She told me of the aunts and uncles and cousins who were killed for being Ukrainian – some by the Soviets, as many by the Nazis.

It was Natalia who got me thinking about a more complicated Ukrainian history, and I eventually found myself enrolling in the Master of Library Science program at Western University. My goal wasn't to become a librarian; it was to learn how to research. I wanted to write books on the topics that I couldn't find in the library.

While some of the things I was curious about and wanted to research were Ukrainian in origin, not all were. For instance, I have always been fascinated with coming-to-Canada stories. I once happened upon the story of a child who had been rescued by Canada in 1923 with forty-nine other Armenian orphaned boys and set up on a farm in Georgetown, Ontario, where they were given schooling and trained to be little farmers. Delving into that one boy's history captured my imagination and sent me on a decade-long quest for information about the Armenian genocide. This was in the late 1980s, and at this time, information on the Armenian genocide was largely suppressed. Armenians themselves would not talk about it for fear of their lives.

The first book I wrote was a five-hundred-page sprawling historical novel for adults set during the Armenian genocide, when an estimated 800,000 to 1.5 million Armenians were killed between 1915 and 1917, a genocide officially denied by Turkey.[3] I shopped it around for a year and got more than a hundred rejections – thank goodness, because like many first novels it was not well-written. The manuscript did attract the interest of a small production company; so my first ever fiction sale was a Hollywood movie option.

During that year of rejections, I wrote some Ukrainian-themed short stories. One was a historical folk tale based on my grandfather's internment during the First World War here in Canada. Figuring I'd get another hundred rejections, I submitted this story to a dozen children's publishers at once. Within two weeks I had three contract offers. Penguin Canada ended up publishing *Silver Threads* as a picture book.

It was not until I was doing my Master's degree in Library Science that I was exposed to children's literature. One picture book still stands out in my mind: *The Paperbag Princess* by Robert Munsch. As an adult graduate student, I was blown away by the maturity of the theme; more than that, I was impressed by the respect the author had for the intelligence of his readers.

I was also surprised to see that the illustrator for *The Paperbag Princess* had a Ukrainian name. It was the first time I had seen a Ukrainian name on a commercially published book. I devoured Munsch's books, carefully examining each one, admiring the artwork. In the back corner of my mind, I vowed that if I ever got a picture book accepted for publication, I would do everything possible to have Michael Martchenko as my illustrator.

Once my agent sorted through the offers and a contract was signed, I convinced my editor to ask Martchenko to illustrate the book, and he did a beautiful job. But as any author knows, getting a book published is only the first step. There are then interviews and book tours, and my publicist told me to expect around two weeks of promotional work, but I found myself still doing interviews more than seven months after publication. I began to feel confident, proud even with this positive reception.

However, the Ukrainian community was not as universally enthusiastic. While many people in the community were thrilled with the book, some told me that I had no right to this story because I wasn't a "real" Ukrainian. Others were incensed because they felt it was undignified for Canadians to know that some Ukrainians were interned during the First World War. Better to bury that part of our history, they said. Others complained about Martchenko's illustrations – in particular the "Soviet" hat on Ivan's head, despite the fact that the era was pre-Soviet and the hat had been drawn from archival photos. Through this kind of feedback, I began to see that for some people there is really only one way to be Ukrainian, one story that can be told. But I was no longer a green undergraduate student, susceptible to shaming.

Maybe I still didn't belong; maybe I still didn't fit in; but I was finding my voice as an author. I rolled up my sleeves and submitted another Ukrainian-themed historical folk tale for consideration, *Enough*, a story of a girl whose ingenuity saves one village from starvation during the *Holodomor*.

Penguin was not interested. The *Holodomor* – the genocide of 1932–3 in Ukraine that saw millions of people starved to death in a man-made famine – was only recognized by Canada as a genocide in 2003, and I had submitted my manuscript to Penguin in 1997. They suggested that I write a simpler folk tale instead – perhaps one with dancing, embroidered blouses, and *perohy*.

I refused.

We were at an impasse.

They halted plans to publish the softcover edition of *Silver Threads*, and I was on my own.

I had become a one-book wonder. My confidence and my voice had faltered; I felt like I didn't fit in. Again.

Among other projects, I took my Armenian first novel out of the bottom drawer and began reworking it. My literary agent advised me that my voice was well-suited to young adult fiction. Up to that time, I had not read many young adult novels, so I plunged in, reading all that I could get my hands on. I was impressed that many dealt with sophisticated topics yet were paced to be page turners. I believe that young adult readers have finely honed crap filters, and they will put a book down if they're not pulled in by the first paragraph. Many are not averse to abandoning a novel the moment it meanders. The trick was to create a nuanced and layered story with memorable characters and grounded in fact but to leave out the parts that people tend to skip over. Could I write like that? The prospect seemed daunting. But my agent encouraged me. I transformed a snippet of my giant first novel into a young adult novel, *The Hunger*.

Just as I had learned that timeless picture books were more sophisticated than most people realized, my foray into young adult fiction taught me how challenging this genre can be. A historical novel "not only takes its setting and some characters and events from history, but makes the historical events and issues crucial for the central characters and narrative."[4] Larissa MacFarquhar writes that "historical fiction is a hybrid form, halfway between fiction and nonfiction. It is pioneer country, without fixed laws."[5] This lack of fixity may mean "anything is permitted," but for others, straying too far from well-known facts is "a violation of an implicit contract with the reader, and a betrayal of the people written about."[6] If this "implicit contract" between author and reader, a contract that sets out certain boundaries for the amount of creative licence a reader will give an author, exists with standard historical fiction, then it is even stronger and more binding for authors of young adult historical fiction. Adult readers trust authors of historical fiction to know the topic about which they write; if they doubt or challenge the author's facts, they can go out and find out details on their own. However, in my experience, young readers ingest historical fiction as history. For me, the responsibility to get things right is tremendous.

A first draft of a historical novel for children or young adults is typically riddled with footnotes and references. Each and every bit of information that I dug up for my novel *Hunger* had to be documented so that the publisher could make sure I had done my homework. If a teen out there was going to read my novel one day as being true (at least about the historical details if not the specifics of the character's journey), then I had shouldered a heavy burden, a burden of trust.

Trust is a delicate thing. It takes a long time to build it, and it can be shattered in a moment. Once shattered, it cannot be repaired.

I knew all this, and still I persevered with *The Hunger*.

When it was published, I took a deep breath, and waited. If the Ukrainian community had mixed feelings about my picture book about Canada's First World War internment operations – doubting my credentials as a Ukrainian "insider," telling a story that some preferred remained untold, and telling a historical story where every historical detail would be under a microscope – then how on earth would my story set during the Armenian genocide be received?

I was pleasantly surprised. The Armenian community embraced my work. At a book launch at the Armenian Community Centre in Markham, survivor descendants thanked me for writing outside of my own culture and letting the world inside of theirs. And as they lined up for books and an autograph, they gave me precious gifts – a photocopy of a grandmother's diary, a map of the killing locations, a precious first edition of *The Georgetown Boys*, a Turkish gold coin from 1915. In short, they provided me with material and inspiration to write five more books on the topic! Because of the attention given to this untold bit of history, Georgetown and the Armenian community were able to stop the original orphanage building from being torn down. It is now designated a heritage site.

Since childhood, I had felt that books would be the way that I could connect, the way I could stop feeling like I didn't fit in. As an adult learning the craft of writing, I came to feel that insight was more and more true.

I continued to find my voice by writing several more novels set during the Armenian genocide, but my mentor and publisher still didn't feel that *Enough* was marketable; it was still too controversial. Sometimes, however, there are forces beyond the market and duties beyond selling books. I was lucky that my publisher believed she had a moral responsibility to publish my book about the *Holodomor*, because no one seemed to know about the Ukrainian famine. With her support, I knew that if I was going to see *Enough* turned into a picture book, I would settle for no one but Michael Martchenko to do the illustrations again. And this time, when the book was released, the Toronto branch of the Ukrainian Canadian Congress hosted a book launch. I felt relief.

But that relief was short-lived.

I had steeled myself for the same kinds of critiques as I had faced with *Silver Threads*, but I was unprepared for some of the critiques that *Enough* generated. For instance, a fellow writer whom I considered a friend mailed me a ten-page screed saying she was breaking off contact with me because I was a neo-Nazi – evidenced by my writing *Enough*.

She said that if Stalin really did kill all of those Ukrainians, they must have done something to deserve it. I thought: *This isn't about whether I'm Ukrainian enough, or whether I should tell this story, or even if I got the facts right; this is a personal attack; this is about Ukrainians as the bad guys.* By now I no longer felt shame at this kind of characterization. I had done my research, even if no one wanted to look at my footnotes. And then things got scary – death threats, spray paint, plainclothes police officer kind of scary.

I felt a lot of pressure from family and friends to choose "safer" topics to write about. But now that I had found my voice and had found topics that challenged me to go digging through history and get into a relationship with readers seeking a glimpse into somebody else's world, with readers seeking to connect, I wasn't about to give those things up. In fact, I wrote a Ukrainian-themed young adult novel, *Hope's War*, about a contemporary teen whose Ukrainian-born grandfather is accused of Nazi war crimes.

Before I knew it, a pattern had emerged in my writing. My Ukrainian-themed books were less well-received than my Armenian-themed ones. Armenians did not see me as an outsider with no right to tell their stories; in fact, various Armenian groups opened their arms to me, making me feel welcome.

In 2010, my book *Stolen Child* – about a Ukrainian child who was captured by the Nazis and brainwashed into thinking she was German – was released and received without the kind of prickly (and sometimes downright frightening) reception that seemed to dog my Ukrainian-themed books.

Stolen Child's 2012 companion novel, *Making Bombs for Hitler*, is about a girl taken as a slave labourer by the Nazis and forced to make bombs. When it came out, the Toronto branch of the Ukrainian Women's Association of Canada hosted a book launch. The room was packed with former *Ostarbeiters*, children and grandchildren of *Ostarbeiters*. No one questioned whether I was Ukrainian enough to write this story. Many former *Ostarbeiters* came up to me: "Thank you for telling my story," they said. I felt proud.

It's been a long journey for me to turn shame into pride; Natalia helped get me started on that journey, but countless readers of all ages have helped me along the way. They trust me to tell the stories that need telling.

I have been asked why my books are marketed for children and young adults. Sometimes I think the answer is pretty straightforward:

It's all in the voice. I write the kinds of stories that I like to read, about bits of history that have been forgotten or ignored. I write them from a young person's point of view because young people have fresh minds. I plunge into the story, and I leave out the boring parts. When you write like this, it's labelled young adult and children's fiction. It does not surprise me that these books are often bought by adults for their own reading pleasure.[7]

Sometimes, I think the answer Philip Pullman once gave works the best: "There are some themes, some subjects, too large for adult fiction; they can only be dealt with adequately in a children's book."[8]

NOTES

1. As with many of the chapters in this book, my consideration of Ukrainianness in the Canadian context cannot be divorced from the forced internment of Canadians of Ukrainian descent during the First World War. I hold a position on the Endowment Council of the Canadian First World War Recognition Fund as the Internee Descendent Representative; my grandfather Yuri Feschuk (George Forchuk) was interned at the Jasper Internment Camp.
2. Any scholar, thinker, or writer who cares about Ukraine – its past, its present, its future – must always, it seems to me, contend with Russia. Euromaidan protests, Crimean separation, and the unfolding drama of contemporary Ukrainian politics make this as true today as it was when I was a student.
3. For more information on Turkey's official stance on the Armenian genocide, see Dixon, "Defending the Nation?," 460.
4. Abrams, *A Glossary of Literary Terms*, 194.
5. MacFarquhar, "The Dead Are Real."
6. Ibid.
7. "Young Adult Books Attract Growing Numbers of Adult Fans," *Bowker*, accessed 5 March 2015, http://www.bowker.com/en-US/aboutus/press_room/2012/pr_09132012.shtml.
8. Pullman, "Carnegie Medal Acceptance Speech."

4 Bringing Back Memory

MARUSYA BOCIURKIW

1. A Conversation

It had taken me weeks. To make this phone call.

A Scotch on the rocks beside me, for courage. I was ready to hang up at any moment. Should the need arise.

My mother's voice, deep and unworldly (she'd had her larynx removed) came on the line. I thought I could hear wind. And crackling electricity. And ocean.

We chatted. The weather. The grandchildren. World affairs. Her latest method for making really good chicken stock. (Use a crockpot). Then back to my food memoir. The book was about to go to press.

A question. I needed to ask.

But first: funny stories about the advance publicity. The live phone interview on national radio. First time I spoke publicly for the book. Me at my kitchen table wearing yoga pants, an old feminist T-shirt (*If I Can't Dance I Don't Want to Be Part of This Revolution*). Held the receiver to my ear, waiting to go on air. I could hear the hosts. Behind them, that wind again. And witty repartee meant to introduce the interview, in uneven staccato. Like the *pock pock pock* of a tennis ball.

Hey didja ever get dumped and then all ya wanted to do was eat burgers and fries for a month?

For me it's ice cream. Every meal.

Oh yeah? What flavour? Vanilla? Chocolate? Rocky Road?

It was entirely possible they had not read the book. The title, *Comfort Food for Breakups*, had been taken literally. What they wanted: self-help. Or me, listing zany things I consumed after I got dumped. What they got: an unfunny story. About the time I stopped eating entirely.

That interview got heard by just about every single person I knew.

I told my mother stories. The long, dark conversation at Terroni's with Marion, food columnist for the *Toronto Star*. Like a forties newspaper woman with her vintage suit and grand, brash manner. *Go. Ahead. And. Order.* she'd said happily, in a plummy British accent: *It's. On. The. Star.* It was the interview you always imagine having. Respectful, thoughtful, giggly at times. Over lightly grilled wild mushrooms dusted with Parmigiano-Reggiano. We talked: about the Holocaust, about her brother's soon-to-be-published memoir, she was in it. The ethical dilemmas of life-writing. We talked about my book. Marion had savoured every single word.

My mother gasped, tsked, in all the right places. We were both foodies. *Gourmet* magazine was our porn. When I visited, we cooked for each other. Her: chicken stew with *perogies*. Me: fried breaded oysters with mashed root vegetables. The food was a text, perhaps more of a hypertext. The food was our long-standing non-linear conversation.

I got to the point.

So. I've dedicated my book to you. Somehow it ended up coming out furtively. Like I was admitting I stole from her purse when I was kid. Which, I did.

Really?

Yeah. Just wanted to make sure it's OK with you. I can still change it.

She was confused now. Not sure what to say. Silence. And then: *Oh. I can remove your name. Nothing's final.*

No. No. It's. Good. I'm. Honoured.

Now *I* wasn't sure what to say.

This was my fourth book. The first one caused quite a stir to say the least. I keep an archive of letters I've received from readers over the years. Let's just say a couple of family missives didn't get filed. Let's just say my Baba, the love of my life, disowned me.

Grace in knowing that nothing lasts
as though peering through the lake's obsidian eye
you saw the crows' wide-eyed terror
the birch tree's urgent nocturnal fluttering
ecology's web
life's swift current
the ebb and flow of love.

My second book, *Halfway to the East*, a volume of poetry, was more sedate. Through it, with it, I grieved the loss of *Baba*'s love. But my mother, after reading it, said to me, rather grandly: *I. Am. Ashamed.*

My family didn't seem to know or care. That I kept writing and publishing. That my books were in libraries. On people's bookshelves. On course reading lists. On amazon.ca. I could have been writing sapphic Harlequin romances and making a small fortune. For all they knew.

(Imagine. Imagine that you write constantly, perhaps even obsessively. About those people, your people. You are widely known but no hero in your hometown. Shame and pride alternate in confusing and dizzying ways.)

Most of my family had not read *"Vichnaya Pamiat* / Eternal Memory." The cycle of poems I wrote about *Baba*, who died between my first two books. Still deeply missed. They hadn't read about how I created family. It didn't replace them. But it gave me a different way to be. They didn't read the poem I wrote about rivers. About my father and grandmother. About a history of migration that pockmarks my own and my family's lives.

Alluvial deposits of memory
contain their voices
and traces of gesture
Baba's girlish laugh
her half-English half-Ukrainian prairie speech
the way my father always wore a hat
and kissed the ladies' hands.

For my eighty-one-year-old Catholic mother, born in a small village in western Ukraine. It had all been a bit of a stretch. Perhaps she wondered: why didn't I write something *nice*? Alternately embarrassed or diffident about my writing. We'd struggled for years.

The past few years, I started to read to her. My stories. While she was recovering from surgery. While I was visiting at Easter. At the end of a long day of cooking and serving food. Her feet up on the coffee table, bowl of chocolate ice cream on her lap. Stories about food, stories about ex-lovers. About the old country, about travelling, about family, blood and not. My stories, her stories. The same, and different.

Love doesn't always appear in a form you recognize. My friends and lovers are family too; sometimes the meals they cook nourish me more than even Baba's endless feast. I am this family's self-appointed bearer of memory, recalling the absent spaces, recording the recipes, searching for the glimmer of devotion, the aroma of happiness, the back beat of bitterness. Between recipes and stories, I will ask myself a thousand times: who owns these memories? If my way of remembering makes it to print, what does it do to theirs?

But I had stopped expecting anything. Calling her, I was prepared for reluctance, disapproval. Maybe even anger.

Maybe. she said, over the phone. Her voice got all dutiful, the good Catholic girl: *Maybe you should dedicate it to Baba.*

Yeah, no. I already did. My first book – I don't think you read it.

Oh. OK. She's relieved.

So. I said. Took a deep and jagged breath. *You're going to love some stuff in the book. And there's stuff you won't love as much.* (I hadn't read her everything.) I sounded like a schoolgirl. You'd never imagine I had three degrees.

Well of course, she said. *That's how it is. Every. Book's. Like. That.*

She has a Bachelor's degree in French literature. Got it when she was in her forties. She was finally getting to use it.

"But also," I said, still the earnest teenager, eager to please. *There's a lot of Tato (father) in it. You'll like that.*

What. Does. He. Have. To. Do. With. Anything? she said. Voice swelling a little bit in indignation.

I couldn't help but burst out laughing. She'd taken ownership. The book was hers now.

Or, perhaps more to the point. It was ours.

2. A Book

It. Brought. Back. Memories. Said my youngest sister Lydia with a sigh.

She didn't say which ones. Didn't say if they were good memories or bad. We walked around my mother's neighbourhood grabbing a smoke on a cold snowy Christmas Eve. She said it quietly, with innocent gravitas. Made me think this was something more than a tossed-off cliché.

In fact I'd heard that phrase from almost every member of my family. *It brought back memories.*

My mother and father had brought nothing from the Old Country. Not candlesticks, not rugs. Not even a tattered Bible or a treasured *Kobzar*. No photographs or documents from before the 1950s. No worn wooden chest, no tattered suitcase bearing the sticker of a steamship line.

This was not an experience that merited memorabilia. And how could you possibly hold on to anything during that journey? Except your own body and soul. Even those did not emerge whole.

I once asked my mother: *What is your earliest recollection?* I hoped for some texture, a sepia-toned image or two. Of life in early thirties rural Ukraine.

I Remember. My. Tato. Going. Away. To. Canada. I. Remember. How. Much. I. Missed. Him. Was all she said.

Loss. Was all she said.

There *were* memories, in unmatching shreds and uneven tatters. Some mention of horse-drawn carts and trains and boats and trains. A very short story, told and retold by my *Baba*. Of arriving by train from Montreal to Winnipeg, en route to Alberta. Flat broke, with two small children. She asked a cousin who met them at the station for a loan. Just a dollar or two. (This in itself must have felt like disgrace.) He put his hand inside his pocket. He pulled out a handful of buttons. It was 1932.

For my father: a concentration camp and then a displaced persons' camp. Occasional, hushed mentions of deportations, slave labour, mass graves.

And so: no family archive, oral or written. No real sense of where we'd come from. I had grown accustomed to this short history. Much like my father, who ever since I was little had declared that he would die fairly soon. I visualized a correspondingly short future. As though our lives had been cut out of a larger cloth. The extra material long since tossed away. Nothing left, ever. To make adjustments with, to patch holes. To extend, or broaden, or expand.

For what it was worth, I had written a few things down. My family didn't seem to mind. Maybe they understood my book as a kind of archive. You choose what you want or don't want in an archive. And the archive itself, as French philosopher Jacques Derrida has pointed out, is surprisingly selective. But it gives you a kind of security. Knowing the archive is there.

They accepted my book first grudgingly. Then curiously, and finally with graciousness.

Like a new member of the family they hadn't expected, but thought they could grow to love.

3. A Reading

Tamara and I, at the Communist's Daughter. A dim, narrow drinking establishment. Corner of Ossington and Dundas. The former Nazare Snack Bar (the sign still hangs out front).

Tamara: dark eyebrows, sharp cheekbones, curvaceous lips. Familiar to me from all the songs and poems of my culture. A classic Slavic beauty.

But here, in this soon-to-be-very-hip neighbourhood: two of us crammed up against the bar with cheap red wine. Tamara's olive skin and dark hair were unremarkable amid the blonde/pale standards of Western culture. Older than her by fifteen years, I felt protective. To her bemusement I am always trying to find someone *nice* for her.

Hey look, that one's cute, I said. Pointed to a woman in her thirties, very debonair, sitting alone in a corner sipping whiskey.

*Shut*up, said Tamara.

She had been to a literary reading I gave a few days earlier. At a bookstore in west end Toronto. I saw her out of the corner of my eye as I read.

My girlfriend had asked me on the way to the reading. *Who. Do. You. Read. To.* I laughed off her question: *I read to you and only you* in an ersatz French accent. She rolled her eyes, looked confused.

But I think I may have read to Tamara that night. Her face open and proud. Out of all of the thirty people crowded amid the aisles of Another Story Bookshop on a cold spring weeknight. She was someone I could say for sure was one of my own.

This, I discovered, is the surprising, grace-filled aspect of writing memoir. It opens doors. Not professional doors, necessarily. Though there had been some small moments of recognition. How to say this without sounding sentimental: it opens doors to people's hearts.

After the reading. A line of people carefully holding my book for me to sign. Shyly they told me. Images and smells that sneaked up on them. Stuff they thought they had forgotten. The Portuguese *bacalhau* their dad cooked on Saturdays. The *borscht* their Polish grandmother made. The aroma of roast chicken they ate at Passover.

A book goes out into the world. It comes back, many months later. It has been reinterpreted, it is a different book. In Edmonton, first stop on my western Canadian book tour. I was met at the airport by my mother and my older sister Jeannie, whom I hadn't spoken to in years. *I. Read. Your. Book. Three. Times*, said Jeannie. She said it with a frown. As though the compelling nature of my book had been something of an inconvenience to her. But then, to clarify: *I actually highlighted the parts I liked.*

The next night, a reading at Audrey's Bookstore on Jasper Avenue. Two blocks from where my grandparents ran a dry-cleaners in the sixties. I counted six family members among dozens of strangers and friends. My mother brought a tray of her baking. (A precaution against whatever store-bought anglo cookies the bookstore might purchase.) She sat in the front row, dressed in a brocade jacket and a long black skirt. White hair gleaming. In the row behind her: Sonya, one of her friends (I call them the Divas of the Church), grey hairdo poufed to perfection. Arms crossed. Mouth set in a grim red lipsticked line.

I was dawdling, waiting for friends to arrive. But my mother, taking charge (the book was dedicated to *her*, after all), ordered me to start. (And later, with the universal "wind it up" gesture, let me know when to conclude.)

As I began to read: a gang of dykes from the university clacking down the stairs. In their flashy print dresses, tattoos, baggy jeans, Fleuvogs and high heels. Goofy apologetic smiles on their faces. My mother glared at them. They filled the last row, a protective margin.

It was terrifying, reading to that crowd. I had e-mailed people passages of the book in which they appeared. Troubleshooting, really. I anticipated all manner of difficulty. I had transcribed their lives. The edges that overlapped with mine.

Memoir, like memory, is an incomplete document. It records, but it also invents. And it reimagines. What happened. What was said. Perhaps most importantly: what wasn't said, or could have been said. Memoir is highly interactive. Its subjects will argue, add to your story long after it's been published. *Baba had an electric stove, not a gas stove.* Wrote my brother Taras tersely in an e-mail. *She was born in 1906, not 1903. Tato's brother was named Taras, not Mikhailo. I was named after him.* Having submitted this errata sheet (which I publish, finally, here), he was fully onside.

That their disagreements were about details. And not about tone, or point of view, or even about my right to tell the stories at all. This was something miraculous to me.

During the reading, I kept glancing at Sonya. One of the Divas of the Church. Her expression hadn't shifted for the entire reading. This worried me. She usually cries, volubly and sentimentally. At any event, minor or major.

I read the final story. Felt relieved when I caught her ostentatiously wiping away a tear.

*

During the time that I was working on final revisions to the book: an odd, unsettling dream.

The table of contents page of my food memoir gets caught in the furnace of my mother's house, setting it on fire. I try desperately to rescue my family. My youngest sister, an infant in the dream, comes running towards my open arms, but then runs past me, and perishes. The only survivors are two distant relatives, whom I hardly know.

I survive the fire. Save only myself. Distant others save themselves. My book, dangerous and all-powerful. Kills my entire immediate family.

I was staying at my mother's at the time. I told her. About the dream. She shrugged. Then fried me butter-soaked eggs for breakfast, buttered rye toast on the side. I made my mother some carrot-apple-beet juice. She told me what she had dreamt. Making food together, in bathrobes and slippers. Made these topsy-turvy stories easier to tell.

I dreamt I was getting married again. I had met this guy. I didn't know him very well. But he seemed nice. The priest from the church in Edmonton was going to officiate.

I laughed out loud. My mom's unconscious – so loose and free! And this amiable guy, about to do a trip down the aisle with my mother. I wondered: *Che vin nash. Was he even Ukrainian.*

My dream stayed with me. Left an almost invisible stain. For a time I wrote carefully. Too carefully. What would my family think? Would the book destroy relationships already brittle with misunderstanding? What about the Divas of the Church? Those notorious high-femme Ukrainian ladies about whom I wrote with love, but also with humour and irreverence? Would they go after me with carving knives and caustic commentary? Would I never eat their home-made cherry squares again?

*

Tamara and I finished our drinks. The bar was slowly filling up. With the twenty-something hipsters who eventually colonize all unfashionable neighbourhoods. Tamara hadn't mentioned anything to me about my reading. But then turned to me and said. *My friend Anna, she is such a fan of yours!*

Shut up, I said.

No you shut up. She told me she took the book with her when she went to visit her father. He's dying. Cancer or something. Anyways, she read to him from your book. The parts where you write about your dad. She said it helped them to reconcile.

I was uncomfortable, for some reason. Ran my finger around the rim of my glass. Glanced around the room. Considered ordering another drink, or going to the can.

Tamara slapped me on the arm.

Ow! That hurt! I said.

See, she said, her brown eyes glowing. *Your. Book. Has. Healing Powers.*

4. A Meal

January 6, 2009. Christmas Eve for my father's side of the family. Old-school. They speak Ukrainian perfectly. They celebrate Christmas in January. They even do that thing where you lay a place setting for the dead.

I have taken two buses and a subway. My cousin's high-rise apartment on the edge of Mississauga. Earnestly, I lug with me home-made organic wild mushroom sauce. Overpriced *rugaleh* from the Harbord Bakery. A pair of fancy shoes. I aim to please.

They've been inviting me for years. I have ignored their invitations for as many years. But this year, this new, fresh year. No time or energy to do an alternative celebration. This year there'd already been some heartache. This year, as though heeding a divine directive: I go.

The bus lets me off. A seventies high-rise somewhere north, or is it west, of downtown. I cross a six-lane thoroughfare. Spotlit by high beams. A lone figure in a brown coat and a bulging black fabric bag. A long driveway past identical apartment buildings. An elevator to the seventeenth floor.

The door of my cousin's apartment opens. To a small living room crowded with cousins from Ottawa, Montreal, and Toronto. And an ancient aunt. The walls covered in paintings. Embroidery everywhere. The group ranging in age from mid-twenties to mid-nineties.

Some of these cousins, I haven't seen since I was little. They terrified me. With their ethnic bravado, their lack of irony or regret. All those years in church basements and graveyards or marching in uniforms.

I am kissed three times by each person in the room. A time-consuming ritual that surprises me with its tenderness.

I can smell buckwheat. Beets. Fish. I hear wind and time and the voices of the dead. Urging us on.

I sense I am in the right place at the right time.

But I'm wary at first. I sit quietly and watch. My older cousin Yurko passes around traditional unleavened bread. Speaks quietly to each person in the room. Wishing them health and prosperity and the fulfilment of their dreams. At that moment, I have no sense of prosperity. No dreams to speak of.

No one seems to mind.

By the end of the evening, after the traditional twelve courses and countless glasses of fine wine. I am laughing along with my younger cousins. The stories and the jokes, most of them at our elders' expense. Are all so familiar, like a sweater you've had forever at the bottom of your drawer. You never wear it, and you'll never throw it away. You might need it, someday.

I enter the kitchen to arrange my *rugaleh* on a plate. *I'm. So. Glad. You're. Here.* blurts cousin Marta. Puts down her tray. Hugs me impulsively, pale small face unfolding into a smile.

No one ever really said: *Don't come*, or, *go away*. You left, or you missed out. Because it was unbearable, to be included in such a way. It had been a problem of translation, and of their not knowing. Perhaps of not even wanting to know.

That night, I thought of my friend Dennis. A gay artist, who said to me solemnly, after he'd visited his family in Newfoundland. *They. Have. No. Idea. Of. The. Pleasures. I've. Had.*

It's that, with the stiff uncomfortable body memory of how much you'll have to edit. You just can't get on that bus.

But there's a new generation. The soft, wry faces of the twentysomethings, Taica and Oleh. Who know, and want to know, so much more than I did at their age. *I. Read. Your. Book.* Says Oleh shyly, but with certitude. *I. Liked. It.*

Food and hospitality speak where words cannot. Marta's *borscht* with mushroom-stuffed dumplings. Lida's Greek fish, her sauerkraut *perogies*. My sauce. Based on my mother's recipe.

A language of generosity. The tentative mingling of cultures.

The folkloric, the traditional, the orthodox. It hadn't been enough in the end. But something grew out of it, or despite it. Or in its place. That something is my writing. That something is you, the reader. Or us. Bringing each other back, into rewritten memory.

5. A Revolution

Language like Honey, Words like Stones

My grandmother disowned me. I tell the stranger. Or rather, I hear myself telling him this. In Ukrainian! The words slip out like stones that need getting rid of. We are spending the afternoon together in L'viv. The stranger and I. It is a warm afternoon. Early May. European tourists everywhere. Many of the women travellers wear flower garlands, coloured ribbons streaming over their shoulders. Catching the light.

After the army tents and stacked cobblestones of Kyiv. This tourism with all of its innocence and ready cash is a shock.

He's not really a stranger. He is a cousin, three or is it four times removed. His daughter found me on Facebook. We are meeting for the first time. I am not sure if he understands me, or I him. It seems he wants to come to my film screening. The name of the film is *What's the Ukrainian Word for Sex*. I translate it for him, clumsily. *I am all for that* he says. I laugh out loud, for the first time in days or is it weeks.

Already, I am nostalgic for Kyiv with its worn army tents. Its holes in the pavement, where the cobblestones were. The memorials for the dead with their flickering coloured candles that somehow keep going even in the rain. And oh how I miss *Maidan Nezalazhnosty* (Independence Square) at five p.m. The smell of woodsmoke from a dozen army kitchens. My final conversations with the buxom women who ran the kitchens with gentle accuracy. *How long have you been here. How long will you stay. Six months. I stay until the end.* They came from Podillia and Zaporozhya and Poltava. They left behind their husbands, kids, grandkids, entire farms. *How will you get home. I have no idea.* They came for an idea, or a dream. They came because enough is enough. Because of corruption. Because *EU is our only chance*. One of them, Halya, said: *When they started to shoot at our students. I could not stay home.*

It's always hard to pinpoint. The beginning of a revolution. In November, Yanukovych had decided (most say Putin decided for him) not to sign the EU association accord. Some say it all began with an Armenian man, Yuri Andreev, who wrote on his blog *let's meet on the Maidan*. Later killed. Or was it the politicians' call to protest. #Euromaidan. Others say the turning point was when the students organized. Like Quebec, only the stakes were higher. Police attacked them, injuring seventy-nine. Thereby mobilizing an entire nation. (*Our students.*)

I'd like to come to your film screening. Says the man in L'viv who is my cousin, or my uncle, I'm not sure which. Now we are sitting in an outdoor café eating walnut torte. On the sidewalk, two young women in *vyshyvanke* (embroidered blouses) sing a folk song in achingly exquisite harmony. A middle-aged man in a Ukraine soccer shirt sells souvenirs. Euromaidan fridge magnets. Flags. Headscarves printed with cabbage roses.

In Kyiv. I slipped like a friend, or a spy, through the Maidan. For the last time. I wanted to say goodbye. To Pani Halya and Pani Nadia. To slip them some money for clothes. Of course they offered me *borscht*. And rye bread. And *salo* (smoked pork fat). The *borscht* contained mushrooms from their *selo* (village). How did they remember to bring the dried mushrooms. The *borscht*: creamy, earthy. Halya ran to the next tent to get sour cream. An entire autobiography in that *borscht*. Like nothing I'd ever tasted.

My cousin, Pan Danylo, is well-known in L'viv. He is an actor for the National Theatre. People greet him, happily, respectfully. We walk slowly like characters in a dream. We go into the shops. I have told him I want to buy a *vyshyvanka*. He knows where the bargains are. *Where is the screening* he asks. *I'm not sure* I say. *I'll let you know.* I say. I unfold a linen blouse heavy with black embroidery. I add almost conversationally *My grandmother disowned me because I am a lesbian.* Why did I tell him this. Because I am full of a complicated regret. Because I like Pan Danylo and I don't want there to be any misunderstanding.

My last evening in Kyiv. I met up with Anna and Annia. Partners. We shared pizza and *deruny*, the potato pancakes I cannot get enough of. We spoke in Ukrainian, Russian, French, and English, a Babylon of miscommunication and recognition. They wanted to know about second wave feminism. I wanted to know where they met and how they live. What they did on the Maidan. November, December, January. Every night after work. Passing cobblestones along the line, to hurl at the riot police. Throwing water onto the dessicated pavement that would freeze and form a kind of barricade. Or, organizing feminist film screenings. Or, self-defence classes. Meetings. Discussions. On the Maidan. With the ladies from the village and the dudes in army fatigues and the middle-class women in fur coats and the priests and the rabbis. With the deadly *Berkut* (riot police) and their beetle-like carapaces on the other side. Now, they are tired. Anna especially. She told me: the Ukrainian government reached a deal with the EU. They agreed to put forward an antidiscrimination bill. Required for EU association. But they would be allowed to omit sexual orientation from this bill.

In L'viv, too, I am surrounded by lesbians. Nadiya, my host, a brooding, brilliant academic. Anna K., and Nina, her friends – funny, charming grad students. They tell me how they took the train to Kyiv, rolled-up banners under their arms. Several times. November, December, January. Nina tells me what she said to her mother: *You can't have it both ways. Join the EU but still be homophobic like the church or the right wing. We want to move forward, we move forward together.*

Pan Yurko and I chat about other things. Going on tour. His theatre friends. His first wife. His second wife. Quite the ladies' man. I am impressed.

Ukrainian rolls off my tongue like honey. Sweet, smooth. Perhaps it had been the shame, holding back the words.

Nadiya has offered to call me, in case the family reunion gets too weird. We have arranged to meet on Ploscha Rynok, the main square.

Disowned, I had disowned my own language.

Ukrainian words tasting like nothing I'd ever swallowed before. (*ell-gay-beh-tay, lesbihka. Hei.*) And words I had. (*Pryvit. Yak spravy, Normalno, vsyo normalno*).

In any case, Danylo knows where the screening is. His daughter texted him. She found it on Facebook. I tell him OK.

Nadiya, who has organized the screening. Tells me later she was afraid. That the venue might get firebombed. But it goes without a hitch. Thirty-five people. I scan the room, a high-ceilinged seminar room at the university, anxiously. No family members. I am regretful. I am relieved. Afterwards we head to a bar that sells Crimean wine. Nadiya and Anna K. want to support this bar. Crimea has been occupied by Russia. The bar will not last long.

I phone Danylo on my cell, from outside the bar. There is sadness and pleasure in his voice. He sounds so much older, over the phone. He was glad to see me. I promise to come back. I promise to catch one of his plays. When I come back.

We drink Crimean wine long into the night. Nadiya, Anna K., and the hip young LGBT activist crowd of L'viv. They tell me stories. Being shunned at the university. Organizing a night of films about sex and getting death threats. Fighting corruption in the academy. What they did on the Maidan. The wine is fruity, smells of summer.

We leave the bar, stroll along streets crowded with tourists. Eating ice cream cones. Taking selfies. We chance upon a group of students having an impromptu demonstration. They sing the national anthem. Many of them hold their cellphones aloft, like beacons. *Sxid i Zaxid Razom! East and West together!* They shout, exhilarated.

Whether it is the wine or the sudden absence of shame. The words fall into place, flow into the sweet spring air.

5 Tuteshni

ERÍN MOURE

It is not a story that can begin, and it has no ending; it is the story of "being from here" and of a place that I can scarcely yet put into words. It is the story of my trips in 2008 and 2009 to Hlibovychi Velkye, near L'viv, Ukraine, the village where my mother was born and where she lived until she immigrated at the age of four to northwest of Grande Prairie, Alberta, her family part of a second wave of immigrants that came in the late 1920s to re-homestead marginal farmlands in the South Peace abandoned earlier in the decade when the price of Canadian wheat fell.

I'd gone the first time to L'viv in 2008 to fulfil my promise to my mother, who had died without being able to satisfy two desires, to see the Panama Canal (strangely) and to return to the village where she was born. I promised to return there for her, with some of her ashes, so she could come full circle in this world, even having already left it. My second trip I made in 2009, in the grip of a mad curiosity that grew from love of this mother, of her values and presence and being, her silent tenacity and gentleness in the face of living things, and from my love of *her* mother Anastasia, who has been one of my familiars all my life. I was also held in the grip of never knowing "where" I was from on my mother's side, because any such "where" had been so shocked and damaged in the currents and aftermath of the wars of the first half of the twentieth century, damaged and then ended with the Second World War and the decimation of three peoples in the "borderlands" of Ukraine and Poland that were terrain of struggle between the colonial powers of Russia/Ukraine and Poland/Austria but were also simply home to people who had lived tucked in that corner for centuries and who still kept their own traditions: Roman Catholicism and the Polish language alongside Greek Catholicism and Ukrainian, often, as in the village of my mother, in the same house, and nearby, a few kilometres away in the town, the community of Jews.

This whole area, in the first part of the twentieth century, succumbed to the roilings of death so many times, roilings carried out under the sign of wars, fascisms, genocides, anti-Semitism, communism, all carried out by people I shall not name here for it is known, and no one now alive did what they did. Suffice to say that, in the Second World War, the link of my own family to the borderlands was sundered forever (or almost forever). What happened to the family was something I already knew, intellectually, and can describe, for the history is a known thing (though denied, silenced, and also clotted into accusations and vituperations both by those who identify with "Poland" and and by those who identify with "Ukraine," to the detriment of the people who live forever where they are and identify with "here"). With the murders and expulsions of "the Poles" by "the Ukrainians" that occurred after the Nazi obliteration of the Jews of Ukraine, and the revenges enacted on the other side, and the official expulsions mandated by the world powers at Yalta as a way of creating ethnically pure states and ending strife (or so they believed, then), a world that was wounded, hurt, struggling, was finally and utterly changed.

Still, as the Galician poet Chus Pato said to me, standing in the village beside me on my second visit in August 2009, knowing there was a huge ache running through me: "People don't live history; they live their lives. History is a catastrophe that passes over them."

Thus it was in the village of Hlibovychi Velkye. Today, though there are so many Humalyaks (my maternal Ukrainian relatives) still there that *someone* must be a distant relation, there are no more Hrandyshi, and no more of the so-called Polish families from the part of the village known as *Storonka*, the other side. In the cemetery, Polish graves that might once have borne my grandfather's family name have all fallen and vanished but for two, both Potecki graves, made more solidly for Poteckis were the magnates, the landowners, the *pani*. By way of explanation, in an explanation that tells everything, the villagers told me, "In other villages, people came back from Poland to tend the graves, but here no one came back to tend them so they fell with the years." Still, no one ever vandalized them, and no one ever built again in the space where the Roman Catholic church had been, where my mother was baptized because – it must have been, for her mother was a Humalyak and in accordance with the tradition, her daughters should have been baptized Greek Catholic, not Roman – the family didn't like the priest for some reason in the other church (not uncommon).

There are no more Hrandyshi but they live on, strangely, in the memory of the old women who come to the road, curious, to meet us, and everyone still knows what part (of the five parts) of the village the Hrandyshi had lived in, and in that place, there is still a small farmstead where people of many names live, generous and quiet people, none of them Hrandyshi, who told me: *We are called Hrandyshi because of where we live. Even people in other villages call us Hrandyshi. There must once have been Hrandyshi here.*

In those quiet words, I found my peace at last, and the end to all my questions that could never be answered. The name of my grandfather, the "Polish" name that had brought destruction and expulsion on all who held it, in that time of turmoil and fear and exhaustion after so many years of war, still lives. Now it bestows itself on the humans who live on the land that was the first landscape my mother was born to.

This landscape I looked upon in August 2009, staring with my own eyes across at the sky and hills and gardens, the geese and the golden dome of the Greek Catholic church that was my grandmother's, and the grove of trees across from it where my grandfather's church once stood, and still does, as trees. *No, Mom,* I said to myself, *you are not from nowhere. You are from here.*

*

Two years later, in the spring of 2011, I went a third time to Ukraine, and with Ukrainian friends from L'viv, Oksana and Taras, generous friends who had mapped the coordinates of the house of Oleks Humalyak, my Mom's maternal grandfather, identified from old property archives in L'viv, we walked down the main road of the village and stood among buildings, different now, sited in the very place where my mother would have first opened her eyes, would have learned to walk. The Hrandyshi may have come from the other side (my grandfather was not a landowner and did not fall into the clichés of what a Polish person was, so there is no record of his home) but the village was mixed, and it was here where my mother grew, and here where she left.

*

When I was a child in Calgary, and an adult in Calgary again when my mother was dying, she told me that people can pray to trees. She had told me as a child of the riches of sugar and medicines that came from the birch trees that grew where they'd immigrated and settled, in the South Peace River area of Alberta. When she died, my brothers and I buried her ashes which remained after my trip to Ukraine among her favourite trees in the high mountains just a few feet from the Alberta/BC boundary. My mother would have to be buried near a border!

Before she died, her priest had told us he disagreed with us having no tombstone for our mother, as descendants will have no place to go to pray. I said: but we think of her when we go out into the trees, for trees are prayers. In Ukraine, in Alberta.

*

All my trips to this Ukrainian "here," to this ancient maternal home, and my entire history as part of this family, are condensed in one photo. It is the photo taken for the passport of my grandfather and grandmother when they emigrated in 1929 from their "here" that was then in a country called Poland: the photo of a family half "Polish" and half "Ukrainian" but entirely and forever from Hlibovychi Velkye, Ukraine. My mother and her sister and her youngest older brother are in that photo too. The oldest three brothers had their own passports, I imagine. But there is something else in the photo as well: it is the very position assumed by whoever holds and looks into its image. In looking at this photo, my eyes irremediably assume the gaze of the photographer in town who framed this picture of two village parents, and the youngest three of six children not old enough for their own passports.

Mine is the gaze of Isak Messer, photographer and printer of Bibrka, the market town three kilometres away from the village. "Some people only shopped at the Ukrainian stands," my mother once told me, talking of the weekly market, "and some at the Polish ones, and some just at the Jewish. But because we came from a mixed village, we shopped at all of them." I remember my mother telling me as a child that, during the war, in the South Peace country of Alberta, on a subsistence farm on the side of a muddy mountain, her parents stayed up at night whispering of the horrors going on back in their home, in the "old country." "We knew what was happening to the Jews." (Bibrka was the site of a large regional ghetto, twice extinguished, once by parading a thousand people through my mother's village to the railway and thence to Belzec – though a couple of hundred people refused to go and were shot in Bibrka for refusing; a second time a year later near Volove, a nearby village, in a pit that ran blood out of a hill and down to the road; and again, in a final spasm, the killing a few days later of the people who had escaped to the forest.) A year later, my grandparents in Alberta knew what happened to their own people, the "Poles" and those mixed up in some way with Polish culture: those who were baptized in the wrong church, for example. Those who survived the new set of burnings by the Ukrainian nationalists and counter-burnings by those who were identified as Poles were expelled scattershot to the west of the new Poland (once the east of Germany), under the terms of Yalta.

Isak Messer's name figures in the Jewish Books of Holocaust Remembrance, the *Yizkor* books, among the many names from the bustling town of Bobrka (the Polish/Russian name for Bibrka), for he and his family died with the others of Bobrka and the area in the extermination of the Jews. He left me a gift, though, Isak Messer did, a work of art, a work that contains and offers his gaze. It is the first and only photograph I ever had of my mother as a child, four-and-a-half years old, in her father's arms, beside her mother and sister and one brother, struggling to escape, a look of stubborn defiance in her eyes that is so familiar to me.

It was only in the spring of 2009, when I was fifty-four, in the South Peace Regional Archives in Grande Prairie, that in a book of local history and memories published in the mid-1990s, I accidentally found another image of my Mom, taken three months after their arrival in 1929. I recognized her (she was not named) only because of Isak Messer's photo. Standing in a white dress and apron, holding a mass card. With her parents and brothers and sister. *Isak, she arrived safely*.

Although today's independent Ukraine is still rife with confusions and the need for new historiography that fully admits all parts of its past (image here: the professor in L'viv who eagerly asked me my family name, then responded flatly and without interest "that's a Polish name," effectively expelling me again from national territory that is just as much mine in memory as it is hers), it does now include as its citizens everyone who lives on its territory. All, today, regardless of background, are Ukrainians. And I am half Ukrainian, of the Hamulyaks of the earth and of the Hrandyshi of the air, the *tuteshni*, the people "from here." I come from people of the Ukrainian earth who trade with and recognize the legitimacy of all the peoples.

I feel compelled and responsible to speak of these things because I can speak. I have grown up in safety and without state-organized terror. My grandparents, though, had been stunned silent by the catastrophe that passed over the place where they were from and which they had loved; their daughter, my mother, in many ways fled this stunned silence of her progenitors. Two generations later, the silence is less deafening, and the "nowhere" of my mother is a place, with a name I can pronounce out loud: Ukraine. For those who could not do so, I returned; for those who desired it, like my mother, and those who did not, like my uncles, I returned. My grief for the cultures of the borderlands that were lost now rises freely out of that great silence that underscored my childhood and was left as a question in my adult life until my mother sent me with her ashes, to give me a gift beyond all gifts, a gift I cannot repay or return, and a gift that lies forever outside the economy of gifts.

At last, in the third generation, I am able to mourn, and admit, and rejoice, and mourn, and embrace, and be present with my Ukrainian and Spanish Galician friends to stand on a muddy road in the trees and honour the village and people I came from, honour what remains and what was lost, alongside them, and honour their sorrows too, for it has not been easy, because here after everything in the world was lost and the world ended, another world went ludicrously and painfully on and they lost even more. I mourn and walk their streets and wish them well, where they live, and I thank them for acknowledging me in some way as one of theirs. *You can come back now.*

Someday, perhaps Ukrainian history itself will be able to say the same and will be able to admit all of us.

In the meantime, I think of my grandparents whom I loved, and my mother, and my brothers, and my friends in L'viv. It all makes sense to me now; not every question is answered, but I have laid aside the vindications to mourn, and I know that my mother comes from *here*.

*

Me as a child of a mother.

I grew up with a mother who came from *nowhere* (because the strife hurt them and their families, and the war and its aftermath finished off the diversity of the country they came from), and it was only after her death that I found out what *nowhere* is and discovered the wounded mixtures of us nobodies.

Now I have travelled and seen, I can speak up and say I have an identification with Ukraine, and then ask out loud that, given this history, how can I and my mother be excluded from definitions and representations of Ukrainian culture promulgated in Canada?

I am a writer. I sit down and I write. And am a Canadian, unhyphenated, as writer Juan Gelman is an Argentinian (his family too were from

Ukraine). These crossings of pathways: I am Québécoise by adoption, Albertan by birth. Ma mère disait toujours quand j'étais petite qu'il y a deux langues au Canada, l'anglais et le français. Je pensais donc que mon grand-père parlait français, car je parlais anglais. Ce n'était pas par méchanceté que ma mère disait ça; elle habitait, elle a choisi d'habiter, le Canada. Sans trait d'union. Elle était férocement canadienne. Peut-être, en partie, elle a voulu échapper la tristesse de ses parents face à la destruction de leur monde. Car leur monde, qui était un monde de paix, même s'il n'était pas en paix, n'existait plus en terroirs ukrainiens, et peut-être n'a jamais existé. Ce "jamais" peut être disputé, discuté, et n'est jamais confirmable, mais le fait que ce monde a été étouffé "à tout jamais" durant et après la guerre est confirmable, et ne peut pas être nié.

J'ai toujours cherché à connaître cette femme, ma mère. Je crois qu'après trois voyages en Ukraine, après avoir vécu moi-même le lieu où elle a vu le ciel et la terre pour la première fois, où elle a appris à marcher et à parler, je la comprends mieux. Pas complètement, car il est impossible, mais mieux. Et j'ai, par la suite, une connection plus forte avec ma grand-mère Anastasie.

Donc je ne suis pas une écrivaine ukranienne-canadienne comme tel. My fundamental identity is not "ethnic," nor am I an "ethnic writer." Mais ma histoire, et maintenant ma histoire écrite et poétique, oui, est une histoire ukrainienne. Nier ce fait serait un attente contre la verité même.

My fundamental identity, if I have one at all, is that of an allergic person. My next identity, once I am sure I survive, is that of a human person, responsible to others. And I have an identity imposed on me, in some ways, for I am gay, lesbian, and thus possess what I have called "a policed sexuality." My work in poetry, on the whole, has always come from a dedication to exploring language's possibilities at its borders, and fraying those borders.

My mother is part of who I am, I now realize, because I have always been a creature of borders, willing to cross borders, of languages, of syntaxes.

I have always been outside "Ukrainian-Canadian identity" and rarely see that identity express a willingness to admit the complexities of Ukrainian history and belongings that Ukrainians themselves admit in western Ukraine. The poets and gym teachers and the meter readers and the theatre people and the people in the village, who said, simply: "You can come back now."

So I have.

Excerpt from
The Unmemntioable

There are persons who can speak no more, whose very names have vanished. Yet a name excised from the verge where it once lived still casts its sound on all who sleep there and enters their throats. "We are called *Hrandyshyi,* for once there were *Hrandyshyi* here …"

I remember the last sound my own mother called out in the city of my birth, in Calgary. A sigh, an interpellation that refused to articulate its word. I turned to her and spoke, as I was meant to.

Language *here?* Blind figuration? Грендиши? *Hrandyshyi?*

There must be some other entry. It is not enough to have a body, so I would purge myself of it. But desire persists me. My mother sitting up in bed and me beside her. The intensity of her blind gaze. How can I talk about the face here? When a border leaves, *I* vanishes. *Máty.*

She carried a lantern out into the field to find her child. Its orange light stroked with hay.

A mother is the unmemntioable boundary
that can never come fully clear.

vanish
endure
[ripple]

Her brother years ago insisted she could not go back. "The village is gone; they burned it in the war." Who knew *who* burned it. A cousin once barred from Ukraine at the border said, "it didn't matter that I could not cross; there is no village."

But the village exists and the woman who walks alongside me on the soldiers' road, on the side of the river called Сторонка, points to where houses burned. The Polish houses were here, she said. And the church across the Davydivka, its grove since empty

She calls this grove not _____ but _____. (I don't catch the words)

We both know what occurred, *the glorious patriotic militia were called to fight the historic enemies of the people.*

(the museum in L'viv decrees it so)

What the villagers call that empty space of weeds, that grove or knoll where my mother was baptized. Not _____, but _____.

Not церква but костьол, *kościół*, the word in the banished tongue

       Shibboleth?   [can't hear you.]

       Ear of corn?   [can't make out the word.]

She coughs. The body's own water pools in the crevice of her clavicle. The wind ripples the lake so shallow now that no fish can winter there.

(I are my own~~enemy~~memory)

[river]
[flick]
[flicker]

Unfortunately, censure has cut history up.

A wide experience by degrees sapped the faith reposed in my senses.

Silence at barbarity <mars> kills our souls in instalments.

The wreck of culture, daughters observed brothers die in <to> great pang.

At first, language was cut off; closer, it pulled out eyes.

There, hope could not know we.

It is possible that all that coincides in the body are merely chimæræ.

In the passport <photo> the child <unstable signifier> defiant in the father's arms <thick hands> stares <outlive>.

"C'est sans doute là où la pensée se trouve."

Monster dozing in a person arises in extreme condition <poetry> and begins ravening. Faces remember people's names. Fear witness what they? Cough smoke from houses, this old church. Murdering <struggling> lasted repeated hours. That they survived <save> miracle.

Humiliation does not justify blood to trail out of skin. Horse reared up in my village. No one humiliated nobody in <to> my village. Different nations lived in agreement by centuries <ages> .
But later part of my village completely crumbled, gone my other <polish> <local>.

Great fragment fallen to abyss and trees for tumulos cut down, pears, apples, forest birches. Therein lies the profound correspondence between the being and the thought.

Who they is. A Möbius problem. The woman in the village, too young to have witnessed, saying: "Ukrainians sent by Stalin built houses where the old had burned." And the official story, said awkwardly. "Stalin sent the Poles to Poland."

Grove of trees:

Asile. Asyljm.
(we never touched or hurt the graves)
the empty grove
(we never touched or hurt the trees)

(i don't know why they did not come back to tend them)
костьол

Volove, Bibrka, forest, <Belzec)>

insert a map of culture here.   [   ]

Je suis moi-même une machine à écrire.

"... Ukrainian," said my mother.
"Polish," said my uncle, older.
"But Mom is Ukrainian," she insisted.
"Polish was what they taught in school!"
"Austrian," said my grandfather, gazing out at the soldiers' road.

"In secret on the mountain I tried to read the letters, for my parents worried awake at night at what they told."
"One alphabet I could not read, they did not teach it in Canadian school."

The Unmemntioable © 2012 by Erín Moure. Reprinted with permission of House of Anansi Press, houseofanansi.com.

6 Putting the *Baba* Back in the Book

DARIA SALAMON

"There needs to be more Ukrainian in this book," my editor says. It's her first order of editing business.

"More?" And here I'd been trying to get rid of much of that Ukrainian. It kept popping up all over the place as I wrote the book. In fact, I thought I'd already edited most of it out.

"Yes, more, more. Those are some of the most endearing parts of the novel."

"Endearing?"

"Contemporary women's fiction tends to be blanched of anything ethnic," she explained. "The Ukrainian-ness is what makes this story original and real. For example, why do you refer to the grandmother character as '*baba*' only a few times? The rest of the time you call her grandma."

Because a couple of those *babas* slipped passed my pen in the vigorous revision process. They're stubborn, those *babas*. I don't bother to tell my editor that all of the "grandmas," in fact, used to be *babas*. *Babas* were scattered all over my book, the way they are at a church bazaar during a game of Blackout Bingo. I tried to banish them from the pages of my novel. There's just something so prickly about that word.

"The relationship Anna has with *baba* gives your protagonist cultural context," my editor enthused. And she went on to tell me about a childhood friend she'd had who was Ukrainian. "I was so jealous of her when I was a kid. She was part of this amazing, rich culture. She was always so blasé about it. Your book brought all of that back."

I could relate to my editor's friend. I certainly didn't tone down the ethnic component of the book because I thought there was something wrong with being Ukrainian or because I'm embarrassed about my own Ukrainian Canadian heritage. Most days I celebrate being Ukrainian Canadian. Who wouldn't want to come from a culture that counts *perohy* as a food group? Heck, in a lot of ways, being Ukrainian Canadian is like winning the cultural lottery. I could go on and on about how rich my childhood was due to the fact that it was infused with so much cultural activity, from Ukrainian dancing to playing *bandura* (albeit badly). I adored two summers spent at the Mohyla Institute learning the language ... and kissing those Ukrainian boys. As a child, I wasn't always overjoyed about being schlepped from one activity to the next, but as an adult reflecting back on it all, I feel like I was privy to something pretty special. Those experiences and my Ukrainian Canadian-ness organically surfaced in the first draft of *The Prairie Bridesmaid* – the draft where I was getting the story down in its rawest form, the draft where I didn't think about market or audience, the draft where *baba* was there more often than grandma.

While my involvement in the Ukrainian Canadian community these days might be a little lacklustre – especially after sporting an embroidered blouse for half my childhood – I still feel very rooted in and proud of my Ukrainian Canadian-ness. As I had that conversation with my editor, I began to see that the problem was that I was *too* comfortable with my heritage. It didn't seem book-worthy. I wanted to write a universal story. I feared if it were too Ukrainian, then only certified prairie Ukrainians who bake their own *paska* out of wheat they've grown would read it. I worried it would detract from the wider appeal of the book. So, in subsequent drafts I worked on softening the cultural tone of the novel. To be clear, my book – complete with edited, neutral grandmas and unedited, stubborn *babas* – was written as a piece of contemporary, popular fiction. It's a funny chick lit novel that is meant to have wide appeal. It's unlike the reams of sociohistorical novels that tell real-life Ukrainian immigration and settlement tales; rather, it tells a story about a woman getting her shit together. The fact that she happens to be Ukrainian seemed to me a distraction that I should probably edit out to make her more universal. I mean, how many international best-sellers or Hollywood blockbusters boast Ukrainians as their protagonists? Could Jason Bourne of *The Bourne Identity* have been named Jason Boyko? Do we ever find out the ethnic identity of Elizabeth Gilbert in *Eat, Pray, Love?* Gilbertski? Gilbertchuk? Somehow they don't quite ring the same. In these contemporary stories, no ethnicity is ever attached to these characters, because the protagonists could be of *any* ethnicity. No, I didn't think I was writing *Eat, Pray, Love* or *The Bourne*

Identity. Although I wish I had. But I was writing something that leaned heavily towards the commercial genre where there seems to be even less tolerance for an ethnic presence.

In terms of theme, context, and humour, my book fits into the genre of something like the film *Bridesmaids* – a funny film about a woman in crisis who struggles to find herself amid friends who are growing up, getting married, and moving on. The film reached a wide audience; it was commercially and critically successful. There is, of course, no cultural reference in this film either.

Ethnic characters in mainstream books and movies are minor characters and villains. They twirl their sinister moustaches and speak in odd accents, and they don't get to be the main characters. The only exception is when the whole point of the book or movie is ethnic. For instance, ethnicity in *My Big Fat Greek Wedding* makes sense, but my protagonist wasn't having a big, fat, Ukrainian nervous breakdown; she wasn't having an ethnic identity crisis. She just happened to be Ukrainian Canadian. I worried that the ethnic component would be distracting, or make the book less marketable.

I'd just completed the first draft of my second novel, *Push*, and was preparing to submit it to publishers. My agent asked me to rewrite the ending, make it less bleak. She said the climate in commercial fiction was such that they wanted happy endings. I wouldn't be able to sell it with an ambiguous ending, she said. In the world of commercial fiction, ultimately I write the book I want to write, but in the editing process I have to consider commercial viability and the mood of the market. I rewrote the ending of *Push*, and I took the *babas* out of *The Prairie Bridesmaid*. It's the reality of what writers sometimes do. Interestingly, with *The Prairie Bridesmaid*, according to my editor, I'd seemingly misread and underestimated the market, and those *babas* needed to be put right back in there.

The word *baba* might feel prickly to me, perhaps because I have one of those *babas* who used to chase me around her farm with a wooden spoon when I was misbehaving. I thought a *baba* would conjure up precise images and a specific ethno-national identity for some readers. My editor took a gamble that this would be a strength, not a weakness of the novel.

Another dilemma surfaced as I worked on this novel: it wasn't simply an issue of language – *baba* versus grandma. The scenes that included *baba* swayed the novel in a literary direction; they were emotionally and culturally candid scenes in a largely offbeat, comic novel. In one scene Anna makes *pysanky* with *baba*, who is going blind. *Baba*'s inability to paint those eggs is a metaphor for her blindness; the patterns on the eggs themselves symbolize the mapping of Anna's relationship to *baba* as well as Anna's growth and her Ukrainian identity. This cultural component created some resonant themes and shifted the novel into more literary territory. This was a problem because, from a marketing perspective, publishers want to market books as either literary or commercial. There is little room or tolerance for books that attempt to do both because any book has only one cover and can only be marketed one way. At the time we were submitting the manuscript to publishers, my agent and I discussed the challenges of placing the novel with potential publishers, and we were clear that this was a book of popular fiction rather than an artsy literary one, even with those more literary scenes between Anna and *Baba*.

Fortunately, I finally found a publisher and editor who were willing to take a risk. (I also received rejection letters from many who weren't willing to gamble on a novel that straddled genres.) *The Prairie Bridesmaid* was still marketed as commercial fiction, but that punchy *baba*, and Anna's relationship with her as well as with her parents, remained intact. Later, they were often cited in reviews as examples of how the genre of chick lit could be elevated. The *Globe and Mail* said, "fearless and independent Baba … is a most interesting and genuine secondary character and another reason one can't dismiss *The Prairie Bridesmaid* as mere fluff."[1] And I had learned there is a tolerance, even a celebration of ethnic identity in commercial women's fiction.

Ukrainian Canadian is an identity that conjures up pretty specific images and metaphors for many people. Early on, I wasn't confident that those images of making Easter eggs or *perohy* with *baba* were congruent with my contemporary story about a woman trying to escape an emotionally abusive relationship (with a man who is not Ukrainian Canadian, by the way). I wasn't confident I'd be able to juxtapose these two worlds. I had slipped Anna's Ukrainian identity into her contemporary life. I wondered if anyone would want to read about it. My friend Shandi Mitchell wrote a novel, *Under This Unbroken Sky*, that was published around the same time as *Bridesmaid*. It's a compelling story about a Ukrainian family struggling to survive on the prairies in the 1930s, with devastating results; the final image in this heartbreaking book is "the graying house and the prairies unfolding."[2] I fell in love with Mitchell's historical novel. It begins with a black-and-white photo dated 1933, and as the novel progresses, we meet an adult brother and sister living on two adjacent homesteads, raising their children and being crushed by the weight of hard work, poverty, discrimination, injustice, and betrayal. Reading this novel with its rich historical details about Ukrainian Canadian homesteading on the prairies, I thought about my own family's history of farming on the prairies – this is the kind of novel I might have expected to write. Ethnic identity anchors Mitchell's book and drives the story. (Literary critics commented on the common use of this backward glance to Ukrainian Canadian history; "a prairie pioneer myth" merges "a regional prairie identity and a Ukrainian cultural identity," wrote Sonia Mycak long before Mitchell's book was published.)[3] Mitchell deftly weaves the Ukrainian Canadian ethnicity of her story with the harsh historical realities of Depression-era farming. Her literary work, with its interweaving of ethnic identity and historical reality, garnered it numerous awards and well-deserved recognition.

While ethnic identity may not be the anchor of *The Prairie Bridesmaid*, it adds depth to Anna's character and provides cultural context for her story. But unlike Mitchell's book, mine is set in the present and lacks the sweeping and epic scope of a literary text. I felt like I was taking one heck of a gamble leaving the Ukrainian-ness as part of my "Bridget Jones-esque protagonist."[4] After all, my Anna lives in contemporary Canada, one alive with vibrant colours and present-day dysfunction, not crystallized in a black-and-white photo of a bygone era. Would my editor be right about a reading public's taste for Ukrainian Canadian-ness in my kind of novel?

When I secured a Toronto publisher, I anticipated keeping the Ukrainian Canadian component of the book muted and diluted. In an interview Lisa Grekul gave regarding the 2003 publication of her novel *Kalyna's Song*, she recalls an agent telling her, "It's a fine manuscript, but the Ukrainian thing is not very sexy, so next time, be Japanese."[5] That's exactly the response that I'd expected from publishers. My experience reading Canadian literature was that Ukrainian Canadians are relegated to starring in immigration stories about breaking the land. I was pre-emptively trying to spare myself an additional reason for rejection.

In a strange way, my experience as a writer wasn't so different from that of the first Ukrainians who came here chasing dreams of a better life. They changed their names in an attempt to distance themselves from their homeland, to fit into this new country, to get a better job. (For instance, when my mother's family arrived in Canada, some of her uncles changed their surname from Wiwchar to Winchar to make the name more phonetically palatable to English speakers.) It took a long time before they could claim their identity and celebrate who they were and where they came from. I was ethnically homogenizing my book so that it would have a decent shot at making it onto the shelves of your local Chapters. By eliminating the ethnicity from my book in order to fit the norms of the commercial fiction genre, I was following the same instinct to fit in and be accepted that my great-grandparents must have felt. I never felt disingenuous about subduing my culture, and I'm sure my relatives didn't either. They still spoke Ukrainian to their children; I still eat *perogies* twice a week. Of course, I know that the moment I start altering my identity or my art for the purpose of fulfilling other's expectations, I am treading dangerous territory. It can become more and more difficult to reclaim what gets lost or hidden for the sake of acceptance.

But I was lucky.

Thankfully, I found a publisher that was willing to take a risk on commercial Canadian fiction that represented a Ukrainian Canadian identity. At first when my editor said those words – "there needs to be more Ukrainian in this book" – I thought to myself, *wow, they really must not be terribly concerned with selling books*. It turned out that they were cleverly intuitive about what Canadians really wanted to read. Even with all those grandmas-turned-back-to-*babas*, the book did make it onto the front shelves of Chapters. Canadians whose names didn't end in -*chuck* and -*ski* read the book, and they embraced its Ukrainian-ness, certainly more than *I* had in the beginning. One of the CBC *Canada Reads* testimonials for the novel said that "the main character is so real that most of us can relate to her."[6] Maybe all those *babas* weren't so bad after all! At book clubs, readers tell me that the Ukrainian component of the book – especially that *baba* (followed closely by the talking squirrel) – is what they cherish most about the book. And I'm told how refreshing it is to read a fiction book about a modern Canadian woman who just happens to be Ukrainian. Especially one who has problems.

Grekul's "unsexy" story about a Ukrainian Canadian girl in a contemporary setting reached a similarly receptive audience. But while the agent Grekul spoke to was wrong about the public's appetite for a "not very sexy" Ukrainian identity and my editor wanted more Ukrainian-ness, the anxiety I felt about those pesky *babas* in the book was very real. Back when I was revising those early drafts, I wondered if it mattered whether the character was called *baba* or grandma. The core story would be the same. *Baba* means grandmother, so is there really any difference? Does it matter?

When my brother told my parents they would be grandparents for the first time, my mother was beside herself with joy at the prospect of becoming a *baba*. It's what she grew up with; it's what she knew; it's what she longed for. Later, I was surprised to learn that my brother was going to have his son call my parents grandma and grandpa. *We* had *babas* and *gidos*, but my nephew would have grandmas and grandpas. When I asked my brother why, he said, *I don't know, baba just sounds so old and unappealing.* I argued that he was robbing my parents of an identity. Yet I had taken all those *babas* out of my book, altering its identity. I started to think that it matters.

In the context of the Ukrainian language, *baba* doesn't sound "old and unappealing." It sounds like *grandma* – albeit one who probably smells of garlic. But when this word is transplanted into the English language, maybe it does feel a little prickly. Especially when that is the only Ukrainian word one speaks. Referring to a grandmother as *baba* on the school playground, when every school friend has a grandma, might make that word stand out, maybe even become prickly. And maybe my brother, who never spoke Ukrainian himself, was sparing his children this – they are one more generation removed from the language than he was. Reflecting Janice Kulyk Keefer's sense of being "betwixt and between"[7] languages, the next generation in my family will weave their way into the spaces between *baba* and grandma. Maybe the generations will move back and forth between grandma and *baba* – owning it, abandoning it, and reclaiming it – the way that I have with my book. And that's valuable because at least it means we are contemplating and thinking about cultural identity and how it fits into our world.

I'm happy to report that my mother is a *baba* to my own two children. As for the *baba* in my book, I finally realized she could be called nothing other than *baba*. And so all those *babas* were back in the book. Ironically, for a writer who feared all those *babas*, the book's dedication reads:

To Babas and Gidos,
   Both mine and Oskar's.

Or maybe it's not ironic at all, because I feel a book's dedication is an author's most honest words, unconnected to market and audience.

So I fretted about all this Ukrainian in the book before it was published. The book was published with all that original Ukrainian Canadian-ness intact, and all of my fears were put to rest upon its release. All is well, right? Well, just as these general fears about audience reception were quelled, I started to agonize about how the heck the Ukrainian community would tolerate the book. It may have made it in Chapters, but what about Ukrainian church bazaars? If those without names ending in -*ski* or -*chuck* enjoyed it, what about those whose names do end in -*ski* or -*chuck*? What would they think?

What was I afraid of? Let's see – the book is laced with profanity, it contains some explicit scenes, the protagonist is a train wreck. And let's throw in a lesbian sex scene for good measure. Like Marusya Bociurkiw's mother, who wondered why her daughter didn't "write something *nice*,"[8] I worried that there was a lot that isn't "nice" in my novel; it's definitely not your immigrant-breaking-new-land book. What good Ukrainian would want to be associated with this filth? It's a recipe for Ukrainian disaster. I was imagining what all those *babas* playing bingo in the church basement were going to do to me. Death by I-27. My own *baba* was blind by the time of publication. I was saved by glaucoma and a slow publication process. I cower with fear to think about what she would have done to me. Even with her limited vision, she's still pretty adept with her pitchfork.

For the second time, I was wrong. The Ukrainian Canadian community embraced *The Prairie Bridesmaid* with its troubled Ukrainian Canadian heroine. I grew up in the Ukrainian Holy Trinity Cathedral on Main Street in Winnipeg. Between dancing, Sunday school, CYMK, choir, and the various Ukrainian associations to which my parents held memberships, my family should have been paying rent to the cathedral. Not long after the publication of *The Prairie Bridesmaid*, I was asked to open the cathedral's Annual Ukrainian Women's Association Spring Tea.

"Really? And you've read the book? And you still want me to open your tea?" I didn't even know what "opening a tea" meant, but that was beside the point. The organizers had read the book. Not only did they accept the novel, they championed it. They loved the idea that a young contemporary Ukrainian woman would grace their bookshelves; I got the impression that this was the book they'd been waiting for. One woman confided in me that she was sick to death of the stories about Ukrainian farmers. No one in her family had ever farmed.

I attended book clubs that comprised Ukrainian women. It was these meetings that I particularly enjoyed because I was able to find out why the Ukrainian community embraced the book. Women, young and old alike, told me that it was a relief to read about this young Ukrainian woman amidst such dark circumstances. Yet she was still making *pysanky*.

The younger women identified with Anna's relationship with her *baba*, but particularly illuminating to me was that the *"babas"* identified with this young protagonist. She was encountering situations that they had experienced fifty years ago but didn't necessarily talk about. Affairs. Bad Marriages. Sisters who had run off. My own *baba* couldn't read the book, so I gave her the abbreviated, squeaky-clean version and she was very proud that I'd managed to write a book and open the annual tea of a church that she'd helped to build. I suspect that even if she could read it – swears, sex, and all – she'd be proud.

I'm glad I didn't die via bingo ball or pitchfork to the head. I'm glad I left all that Ukrainian in the book. I'm criticized by *baba* about my inability to speak Ukrainian properly – or at all, really. I'm pestered by my mother for not regularly attending the church where I'd spent so much time as a child. But I feel like I wrote a damn good book that celebrates what it means to be a Ukrainian Canadian woman in the world today, even with all her swears, complications, and contradictions. Perhaps especially with all that.

NOTES

1 Robertson, "Marriage à la (Winnipeg) Mode."
2 Mitchell, *Under this Unbroken Sky*, 351.
3 Mycak, *Canuke Literature*, 55.
4 Robertson, "Marriage à la (Winnipeg) Mode."
5 Wawryshyn, interview with Lisa Grekul, 8.
6 CBC Books, "Reader Recommendation Round Up: October 17, 2012," accessed 5 March 2015, http://www.cbc.ca/books/canadareads/2012/10/reader-recommendation-round-up-october-17.html.
7 Kulyk Keefer, "Language Lessons," 23.
8 Bociurkiw, "Bringing Back Memory," 75.

7 The Gulag, the Crypt, and the Gallows: Sites of Ukrainian Canadian Desire

MYRNA KOSTASH

But how about desire? ... which equally can turn the nape of your neck or the back of your hand into a sexual explosion.

Judith Williamson[1]

1. The Doomed Bridegroom

In 304 CE, the Doomed Bridegroom bleeds to death on the hard red earth of the Roman baths, his breast ripped open by a centurion's spear. He is Great Martyr St Demetrius of Thessalonica, martyred during a last, savage persecution of Christians in the Roman Empire. (Not a decade later, Roman emperor Constantine will issue an edict proclaiming imperial toleration of the Christian faith.) In 1885, the Doomed Bridegroom, his face masked by a black veil, slumps in the noose of the gallows at Fort Battleford, North-West Territory, Canada. This bridegroom is Plains Cree war chief Wandering Spirit, and the rope has snapped the back of his neck, trapping there his fluttering soul. (Fifteen years later, my paternal grandfather will take out homestead title in Alberta.) In 1985, the Doomed Bridegroom is dying in isolator cell number three in the fifth year of a sentence to penal servitude, in Special Regime Camp VS-389–36/1 near Perm twelve hundred kilometres east of Moscow.[2] This one is Vasyl Stus, Ukrainian poet, in the Gulag. (Perm-36 camp will finally be closed two years later, in a period of Soviet *perestroika*.)

Stus "completed" his sentence in the grave dug into the tundra floor of the campsite; the place marked by a small wooden stake and the number nine. When he was disinterred by his son four years later, his shroud fell away in tatters, and we catch a glimpse in the wavering video image of the torque of a blackened, leathery wrist. Wandering Spirit's body was tipped into a wooden coffin, locally crafted, and buried in a shallow trench with his fellow convicted rebels, well beyond the walls of the fort, like so many excommunicates outside the cemetery gates. St Demetrius's grave is unknown.

The "doomed bridegroom" is a marginal man, ethnically, politically, historically, and spiritually, exiled to the margins of the dominant narratives of Western Christian Enlightenment and Imperial cultures. At the same time, he is specific, located in dramas of courage, despair, and failures in countries or territories wracked by a complex of cultural and political history, men of a certain "otherness" whose birthplace, language and alphabet, folksong, ancestral memory, and visions are themselves triggers of my erotic imagination.

The Doomed Bridegroom is also a prisoner of my text. I make him up; or, rather, I insert myself imaginatively into the historical record in order to participate in his drama.

What is that drama? A young man, dedicated to resistance against agents of violence and empire, is crushed by them, and then condemned to death. His vitality and passion are still so fresh and muscular in him, leaping through his blood, so that he cries out in disbelief at his own extinction. But this Ukrainian Canadian woman stands as witness, and the story rewinds, and goes on, this time with her in attendance.

In this way she displaces herself from her white girl's humiliation in the Euro-Canadian middle class, where she has been dumped as part of the problem not the solution by those with whom she is most ardently in solidarity.[3] She has eloped with the Doomed Bridegroom to other sites of identity.

I stand in Stus's living room, with his wife and friends, increasingly besotted with jealousy. In my hands, a plate of bread, sausage, and radishes, while everyone else gets drunk and kisses each other in sheer admiration. Even as I create the scenes in which to place myself as admirer, archivist, and chief mourner, I confess guilt of the crime of all erotomanes: lust for the singer not the song. I can imagine scenes from the life, as in this living room. However, Stus's language, his poems, are of the densest linguistic obscurity. I am not admitted there, and so I insinuate myself instead into the cramped living room, its walls foreshortened by bookshelves, I jump onto the Turkish carpet with the dancers, then, gripping the neck of a vodka bottle, I shove myself into the corner of the divan, hip to hip with the poet whose head I pull back with a fistful of his hair, and tip a small stream of the liquor into his open mouth.

Like this, Stus resembles my first lover, in the photograph I took of him in the kitchen of his Edmonton flat. He is in profile, with planed cheekbones and tousled chestnut locks, meditatively considering a large open canister of ground coffee. We would roll together on the slab of foam mattress in the bedroom, crumpling under our flailing limbs the typed sheets of paper meant for the alternative Marxist-Leninist broadsheet, a pedagogical adventure among the masses. My lover was an American Jew, a draft-resisting man from the Bronx, a Communist with a grandfather in a deli – a detail: the wooden barrel of dill pickles at the back, which links for me with a memory of my *Baba*'s crock of sauerkraut in the root cellar – and my lover would eventually abandon me, and the bedroom, and the kitchen sink, for a penitential turn in prison in California. He wasn't for marrying. He was doomed to live out the drama of class warfare in Amerika – which had sent so many of his class brothers to die in flames in Vietnam – in which he laid his body down.

In fact, he did marry, after serving his sentence. But this is the coda, not the tale. Last seen, he was reportedly "bald and very wide."

My last view of him was in the prison yard in 1977, his tough, browned, muscular body in a regulation short-sleeved brown polyester shirt, the chain-link fence the backdrop to our little picnic under the watchtower. I had shopped so carefully: organic strawberries, cream cheese, peppercorn crackers, papaya juice. I moved and gestured with extremest delicacy, so that this moment should not collapse from the reverie in which I submitted ecstatically to my fate as the bride of a man in jail. I would marry him, I swore, restored magically to the virginity at the portal of carnal knowledge, which I had once brought to our bed (that foam mattress), and I would repeat ritually, in the narrow cot of his cell, the first act of my body's sacrifice to the doomed bridegroom.

(It did not occur to me until a couple of decades later that there could have been something problematic in the coupling of a Jew and a Ukrainian who otherwise understood themselves to be stateless children of the Revolution. It did not occur to me that we had prehistories that were slung in our baggage, true genealogies of incrimination.)

I stand in St Demetrius's underground cell. A little light seeps through the chinks of the bricks, so he can see the rats and the crawling things, but I can see the radiance shimmering around his head. His only representation among us now is of this iconic, virginal, celestial beauty sheathed in light, disembodied within his cloak, but in 304 he is still flesh and blood, a youth who, before he was flung into this pit, careered exultantly around the stadium with horse and chariot, leaned forward on the banquet couch for the flask of Macedonian xinomavro, then, sober once more, returned to his villa to join his household in the secret prayers of the late third century Christian faith into which he wished to be baptised: "We praise thee Father; we thank thee Light in which there is no darkness. Amen."[4]

Unknown to history, elusive in the Church's martyrologies, Demetrius is nevertheless protean in the popular narratives: rhetor in the forum of a Late Roman city, aristocratic, charismatic, and pious; folkloric patron of the souls of the dead on his Soul Saturday throughout the zones of Eastern Orthodoxy; to the Bulgarians, miraculous redeemer of the oppressed nation; to the Greeks, warrior saint on the battlements of Thessalonica where my Slavic relatives, in perennially fruitless siege, slithered off the scaling ladders at the walls to their deaths. In fact we can be sure of none of it, so I make him a Christian slave in a Greek household, still young, beautiful and condemned to be among the untimely dead. (Yet – oh holy paradox – the day of his Passion is also his birthday, his first day of his new soulful life.) He dies under torture, his body is hurled outside the city gates to rest among the weeds, and the beasts carry off his bones. If he had a script, it has not come down to us. There is the singer; imagine his song.

Wandering Spirit, Cree buffalo hunter and warrior, a charismatic figure at the peak of his power, rode the plains in an increasingly desperate search for the means to sustain his people after the disappearance of the great bison herds and, after the signing of Treaty Six in 1876, their confinement on the reserves. He had a vision, a vision of his own homeland restored once all of the whites were gone, turned over, released, to their armies and their government, and taken somewhere far, far away, back where they came from. He had his visions, he prayed, he danced and drummed, but nothing, not even a war chief's power, his gun, his coups, his Blackfoot scalps, could alleviate the suffering of his people. Instead, he and his wild young men, the young warriors, killed nine unarmed white men at Frog Lake, now in Alberta. Wandering Spirit died in a mass hanging, was buried in a mass grave, and now lies pressed under the weight of a great stone. His gaping mouth is speechless. The past is now inscrutable to him: blinded by earth, he cannot see ahead. But I can.

Wandering Spirit left no text of his own. But a text was left, by a woman, the teen-aged Eliza McLean who had been his hostage for two months.[5] *Eliza McLean, c'est moi.*

> I'm almost seventeen. I'm useful, good at things. I can shoot, hunt. We won't always have to hide in the bush. Let your people surrender but you and I, we can head north, there are horses at Cold Lake, we can keep on going, north. I'm not afraid of the land, I'm good with babies. I can bear babies [sweeps hands across belly].
>
> [Wandering Spirit shakes her]: Stop this! I have wife and children.
>
> I don't care. Give them to other families. Give them to the church. But take me.[6]

2. Questions Arising

These three Doomed Bridegrooms have been central figures in three of my books – Stus in *The Doomed Bridegroom: A Memoir* (1998), St Demetrius in *Prodigal Daughter: A Journey to Byzantium* (2010), and Wandering Spirit in *The Frog Lake Reader* (2009) – and also in the 2011 playscript *The Gallows Is Also a Tree*. They were all men ill-fitted to their times, the dissident figure confronted by the implacable machinery of the state. Their victories, such as they were, were all posthumous. After the marginalizing and silencing of Indigenous Canadians under colonialism, Wandering Spirit's alternative narrative may be reborn in urbanized resistance movements. Stus has been rehabilitated, disinterred from the Gulag tundra and reburied by an independent Ukraine. St Demetrius is venerated by a triumphant, globalized Christianity. Perhaps Wandering Spirit's last words in the play, a speech I give him from beyond the grave, may serve for all the Doomed Bridegrooms, if they could see through the darkness of the pit:

> I died at 8:27 o'clock in the morning. I could hear the chanting of my people, some far out on the prairie, as the hood was drawn over my head. The priests chanted their own prayers. And then, at last, there was total silence except for the squeaking of the ropes on the gallows' boards. Then our wives began to wail. But no, it was not in total darkness. Even through the hood I could see the sun. *Anohc e-pikiskweya nitapwewin.* Now I am speaking my truth.[7]

Of the three men, only Vasyl Stus shares a time and ethnicity with me. In fact, in all my years as a Ukrainian Canadian writer, I didn't find a project among modern Ukrainian topics until I engaged with the narratives of the dissidents of the 1960s and 1970s.

Through Stus, I imaginatively attached myself to the dramatic narrative of Ukrainian resistance to Soviet power in the politically and ideologically frozen decades of the 1960s and 1970s in Soviet Ukraine. Given my own work on the history of my Canadian generation in the 1960s, it was inevitable that, when I finally embraced the roots of Ukrainian Canadian identity in Mother Ukraine, I traced them through a man of the *Shestydesiatnyky* [the Sixties People]: until then, feline *guerrillero* Che Guevara had carried me off, away from the Ukrainian Canadians. In my pantheon of heroes, all other masculine political "types" are unsexed. With St Demetrius, in my attachment to the form of a tragically young martyr to the cause of the early Christian *eikoumene*, an attachment mediated ambiguously by the Liturgies of the Church, I re-entered a community I had abandoned as an adolescent, the Ukrainian Orthodox Church of Canada. Even so, it is he whom I have chosen, not the Prophet Elijah, say, usually represented as a wild-haired and wild-bearded denizen of the desert, seated forlornly among heaps of rocks, nor Martyr Polycarp, who died an old man, albeit ecstatically, stabbed to death when the flames of the pyre failed to kill him. As for Wandering Spirit, the apparent hopelessness of his struggle, the futility of it, even while he raged against the white men with their railway tracks and field cannon, drew me to him, and not, say, to Big Bear, venerable peace-maker, or to Poundmaker, the strategist who "logically" surrendered. Poundmaker did not hang.

I have made the circuit from Two Hills in western Canada, to the Ukrainian SSR and Eastern Bloc Europe, to Thessalonica in Byzantium, and back again to the "ancestral" western Canadian prairie lands of Cree and Galician contiguity. However, compared to my study of a kind of *sui generis* Ukrainian Canadian-ness in *All of Baba's Children* (1977), in the Wandering Spirit "project" I account for the immediate prehistory of that identity in the history of Aboriginal anguish – Wandering Spirit was hanged in 1885 – embedded in the very land that my grandparents would claim by homestead title in 1900. Note the proximity of these two dates: it is not an uncomplicated account.

Baba and *Dido* had their way with the land – and would be celebrated by their descendants as heroic sodbusters on "free lands" – while the Cree were relegated to reserves. The Saskatchewan poet Andy Suknaski once wrote a poem after visiting me at my log shack on 160 acres of land near Two Hills, Alberta, which I called "Tulova" after my paternal grandparents' village. The poem is "Tulova/1979": "*tulova*, that final peace with spirit and earth / she naming it after that *selo* her parents left in *ukraina* / she buying it with hardearned writer's money / remembering the sacrifice it took / to turn horizon and forest into something / of remembered steppes."[8]

There are several things "wrong" with this picture: my parents were Canadian-born, my grandparents did not come from the steppes, and the only "remembered sacrifice" evoked is that of the settlers at their back-breaking labour where "horizon and forest" are apparently unpopulated. Suknaski does not spend time here in nursing guilt about the vanishing of Aboriginal peoples from the scene in order that the land accommodate Galician farmers, although he is remarkably compassionate towards men such as Sitting Bull and Crowfoot in his classic collection, *Wood Mountain Poems*. Guilt, perhaps, is not the point: what the settlers have wrought is irreversible, and in any case their ghosts demand to be honoured at the family shrine. No, the point, Suknaski seems to be saying, is that we should be mindful of the memory of the antecedent ancestors who had walked this land, with the names for places and heroes and gods, millennia before ours ploughed it up: "... i stand here listening for the possible / ancestral voices / as the wind passes rustling / the rosebushes and taller grasses / by the creek / and i try to imagine who passed here so long ago / possibly becoming this dust / i breathe,"[9] a symbolic Eucharist, consuming the fallen gods gone to dust in the *chernozom* of the prairie.

Or, in the case of the Doomed Bridegroom who is Wandering Spirit: desire in the place of guilt. He did not leave a text of his own but he can be traced in the dramatic if naive account of his teenaged hostage, Eliza McLean, who, I am convinced from multiple readings of her narrative, was in love with this warrior whom she observes at the moment of his maximum potency. He is hated and feared by his enemies, Blackfoot and European, but this is of no consequence to the young woman, herself of mixed Scottish and Cree ancestry. If anything, this has made him even more admirable in her eyes.

In my playscript *The Gallows Is Also a Tree*, I have the older Eliza, in her forties, address her young self, Liza: "But you, you wrote that he was 'quite different' in appearance from the other Indians, that he had 'wonderful,' 'transfixing' large black eyes, and 'jet black hair' that hung in waves down his back. There he is, preparing for the battle at Frenchman Butte, those 'strange' flashing eyes of his again, circling the camp at a mad gallop, 'shouting the long war-cry of the Crees' and waving around that damned Winchester. His curly black hair 'tossing in the wind.' Except for breechclout and moccasins and the cartridge belt across his chest, wonderfully naked."[10] It is meant to be a rebuke to Liza, the fantasist of youthful but doomed romantic love, but Liza wants no other man, however suitable: *E/liza McLean, c'est moi.*

The Doomed Bridegroom is also a metaphor for engagement with history and the historical matrices of my identity. My relationships, my love affairs, with these Doomed Bridegrooms, are a way of projecting myself into the irrecoverable past and to enlarge for myself a prehistory and a history: it is a historical memory project. But "history," I seem to be suggesting, is elsewhere. Or, perhaps, my powerful identification with the violence and complexity of the particular times and places of my Bridegrooms is an acknowledgment that the roots of very brief residency of the Ukrainian Canadian in the New World are too shallow for tragic or epochal history, the only kind that art draws itself to – an acknowledgment that these roots lie in the "chernozom" of Ukraine's recurrent suffering, in (Orthodox) Christianity's bloody beginnings, in the suppression of Cree social, cultural, and economic agency that prepared the way for my being "at home" in Canada.

None of these eroticized heroes is a Ukrainian Canadian, which suggests that my ethno-literary psychodramas occur in a deeper layer of consciousness, chronologically and thematically. To excavate these deeper layers, I have used archetypal "lost loves" in the Ukrainian political and moral drama of the twentieth century, in the contest between Aboriginal and Settler on the vast lands of the great plains a century earlier, and in the medieval mission of Byzantium – the matrix of all Ukrainian identities – among the Slavs. But the archetypes need not be Ukrainian at all: political and moral dissidents can also be Poles, Jews, Greeks; Byzantines can also be Bulgarians, Serbs, Macedonians; the hero indigenous to the prairie can be Blackfoot, Dene, Tsuu T'ina, Assiniboine.

There is an unregenerate heterosexuality at play in the relationship of narrator and lover. I write from the feminism that has analysed and theorized the *material* politics of sex and gender, and built a case for the liberation of women from biological necessity, and against the essentialist-feminist notion that the act of coitus, and not society or history or economics, is the source of women's subordination. My young self was a desiring self who admired and lusted after revolutionary men (as they were then constructed): "earthy men, men of action ... who exert power, occasionally demonstrate self-knowledge, and display proud, peacock-like loveliness," as Miriam Edelson described labour union activists.[11] "What I remember is being always, almost without a break, in love with such men." Like Edelson, I "need not intellectualize this." Think of the physiognomical perfection of the leonine-headed Che on posters in left-wing bedrooms around the world. Think of the fully realized, superb corporeality of Wandering Spirit's warrior body, of Stus's shrinking, obstinate, slave labourer's body, St Demetrius's dematerializing icon body. They are all homes for the transcendent rebel spirit knocking hard against the bars of its bone cage.

Yet the tales of the Doomed Bridegroom also tell the story of my celibacy, a kind of perpetual virginity. His is a free spirit, beyond the reach of the claims of intimacy. I can't have him but he can't have me either. In fact, I am aroused by his unavailability, which offers only elusive and transient couplings snatched from the agenda of his higher calling. He is of no "use" to me as a free man dominating his situation, as in marriage. As I wrote in my Preface to *The Doomed Bridegroom*: "His lovers are thus spared that detumescence in the 'calm of coupledom' that British feminist Elizabeth Wilson predicts, in *The Left and the Erotic*, is the conclusion of more sensible love-affairs."[12] Admittedly, there may be a certain sadism at play here, eroticism associated with the suffering and death of a beautiful man, but no more so than in the apparently salutary Christian meditation on the arrows of martyrizing desire piercing the flesh of St Sebastian just above the border of his loin cloth: "Like the Virgin, his point is that he is pierced but pure."[13] I leave him as I found him.

3. The Genre

Each life is an encyclopedia, a library, an inventory of objects, a series of styles and everything can be constantly shuffled and reordered in every way conceivable.

Italo Calvino[14]

And so I have been drawn over and over again, in sympathies of desire, to heroic figures in the extremity of resistance and sacrifice, in an obsession for narrating, in what I have called "nonfiction tales," a personal history of arousal by historically transgressive men. In some cases, as narrator, I have been compelled to refashion the men's stories in order to make them compatible with my obsession; this refashioning or "making things up" is, controversially, commensurate with the techniques of creative non-fiction, a genre that has suited me well, the literary equivalent of false memory syndrome.

This may be too blunt. During the recent controversy (2006) provoked by the revelation that American writer James Frey's memoir, *A Million Little Pieces*, contained a great deal of invented or fabricated material (in fact, it had been written as a novel), there was a flurry of argument about the ethics of "making things up" in non-fiction texts and of applying fictional techniques to documentary materials. For example, in the newsletter of the International Association of Literary Journalism Studies, Walt Harrington asserts that "truth may be many things – but it is not nothing at all"; nevertheless, he concludes that "truth" consists both in "documentary, physical reality" and in "the perceptions we have of it."[15] A hybrid, if you like. Luc Sante, the American essayist and critic, in a letter to the editor of *Harper's* magazine, defends the non-fiction writer who is not a "reporter," to whom "the truth is a fluid and mercurial thing."[16] Historically, the term "creative non-fiction" seems to have emerged in order to describe what was happening in the memoir and personal essay, genres that no longer relied on linear chronology and fact-checking for their truthful effect. In fact, the whole point of the genre has become to interpret (or even misinterpret) the "given," to submit it to point of view, memories, and contemplative self-examination, to juxtapose "the facts of the world" with "the facts of literature."[17] Some writers have gone so far as to dismiss the quest for truth as a "fetish" that disrupts the kind of truth-seeking that yields its goods "by *not* attending to facts."[18] That is, by attending to absences, to the lost and forgotten, to erased and gone-missing texts and testimonials.

I also note the repeated theme in my work about the Doomed Bridegroom of his textual inaccessibility – Stus's impenetrable, to me, Ukrainian language and perished poems, St Demetrius's biographical ambiguity, Wandering Spirit's orality – which offers me the possibility of creating substitute, alternative, or even wholly original texts to take the place of absence and elusiveness. So Stus the inaccessible poet becomes a man of action, of situations and incidents, in which I move him around and occasionally meet up with him myself; and St Demetrius the inaccessible saint acquires a wholly imagined hagiography constructed from research documents; and Wandering Spirit, whose Cree-language texts were written on the wind, becomes a loquacious and eloquent man of many English words in a playscript in which he and I meet in my time, not his. None of this is gratuitous. The first version of the Stus essay, "Inside the Copper Mountain," appeared in a collection of creative non-fiction, *Why Are You Telling Me This*, that bore the telltale subtitle, *Eleven Acts of Intimate Journalism*.[19]

Journalism: documentation, of the world beyond the private self. The authority and urgency of the actual world, of the lives of others, and of public affairs as they shape our lives, remain the point of departure of my non-fiction. I have always made the case for the Doomed Bridegroom that my obsession with him is prefigured by earlier obsessions with politics, history, and culture in which I am embedded as a woman with a history of my own. I am not a writer for whom everything is subjective, nothing is generalizable.

But I drag him as a collaborator into that history and that autobiography: thus the intimacy. There is an "I" here, a subject, a creature with her own prejudices, passions, and anxieties who is "gathering the news." She is present, so to speak, at the scenes she is describing. She doesn't try to hide.

It is not astonishing to claim anymore that "facts" are often in dispute as uncertain, contradictory, and even unreliable. With each delineated point of view, every story comes into contention with all others. But in this very contestation there is a basis for discovering a new truth. "Their fragmentation, their unreliability, is the basis of their truth ... And the same holds true for any story that touches on a national taboo, secret, mystery, any event that's gone unstudied, undiscussed, unacknowledged."[20] The stories that emerge from the self-examination of a Ukrainian Canadian woman on the prairies, a feminist and socialist, schooled in the 1960s, and living the writing life in Edmonton, are or have been marginalized, unstudied, and unacknowledged, and subjected to the communities' taboos, whether of ethnicity, gender, location, or ideology. They are the ideal subject matter of a genre itself "unreliable" but revelatory of truths undreamed of elsewhere.

NOTES

1 Judith Williamson, "Seeing Spots," *City Limits*, 25 March 1983, quoted in Eileen Phillips, *The Left and the Erotic*, 33.
2 The online resource, *Gulag History*, shows a photograph of Stus (unidentified). See "Dissidents," *Gulag History*, accessed 5 March 2015, http://gulaghistory.org/nps/onlineexhibit/dissidents.
3 Kostash, "The Shock of White Cognition."
4 Nibley, "The Early Christian Prayer Circle."

5 McLean, "The Siege of Fort Pitt," "Prisoners of the Indians," and "Our Captivity Ended."
6 Myrna Kostash, *The Gallows Is Also a Tree*, unpublished playscript.
7 Ibid.
8 Suknaski, *The Name of Narid*, 45.
9 Suknaski, "Indian Site on the Edge of Tonita Pasture," in *Wood Mountain Poems*, 79.
10 Kostash, *The Gallows*, unpublished.
11 Edelson, "Letting Go of the Union Label," n.p.
12 Kostash, *The Doomed Bridegroom*, iv.
13 Darwent, "Arrows of Desire."
14 James-Dunbar, "Authenticity and Textual Violence."
15 Harrington, "The Writer's Choice," 11.
16 *Harper's Magazine*, January 2008, 7.
17 Batuman, "Get a Real Degree."
18 James-Dunbar, "Authenticity and Textual Violence."
19 Kostash, "Inside the Copper Mountain."
20 Wexler, "Saying Good-Bye," 29.

Conclusion: Ukrainian Identities On(the) Line: Writing Ethnicity in a Time of Crisis

LISA GREKUL

On 20 January 2014, after a five-day visit from my parents, I posted a series of photos on my Facebook page that featured my daughter, then about eighteen months old, in her booster seat and high chair, sniffing garlic and eating cabbage rolls. Her *gido* had taken the photos and her *baba* had made the *holuptsi*, hands down my kid's favourite food. She ate nine that day, breaking her previous record of seven, which seemed to me an achievement worth broadcasting to my four hundred or so online "friends." I shared eight photos in the album I titled "Our Little Ukrainian Girl."

Two days later, news broke of the first Ukrainian protesters killed in Kyiv's Independence Square. And, like many of us who had been following the mounting crisis in Ukraine (beginning in late November 2013, when then-President Viktor Yanukovych severed trade ties with the European Union, sparking protests in Kyiv by anti-government/pro-EU demonstrators), I learned about the deaths of Yuriy Verbytskyi, Pavlo Mazurenko, and Serhiy Nigoyan on Facebook.

It took me a few days – not long, and at the same time, too long – to notice the timing of my Facebook post. I couldn't have known what would transpire in Ukraine forty-eight hours after I posted the photos of my daughter, but there was, nonetheless, something obscene about my decision to do so while Kyiv burned. I found myself staring at those photos, and at the date on which I'd posted them, and cringing, and asking myself how I could have been so egregiously narcissistic as to think it appropriate to parade my kid's ostensibly Ukrainian identity in the "virtual" world of the Internet while real Ukrainians were locked in a life-and-death struggle for control over their identities.

To let myself off the hook, I tried to tell myself that Facebook, as a "genre" governed by its own (albeit unspoken) "rules" and expectations, invites the sharing of wildly dissonant information. The logic of the site is such that it's perfectly okay (I mean, people do it all the time) to post a link to an article or video or petition related to mass killings, or political upheavals, or the horrific abuse of animals, and in the next breath to share the details of a particularly rigorous workout, or an exceptionally good meal, or an especially cute kitten (or dog, or goat, or baby). Indeed, as a record of all that we think and do and wonder about and love and fear and hate, Facebook not only permits but, it would seem, requires that we share everything that crosses our minds or paths: our worries about the proposed Enbridge pipeline, our best recipes, the results of the latest quiz we've taken, the kidnapping of two hundred Nigerian schoolgirls, the outcome of our home renovations. *People do it all the time.*

The problem is that, in the days and weeks after the first Ukrainian protesters were killed – followed by many more – I said nothing about Ukraine on my Facebook page. As the Euromaidan death toll rose and rose, and Yanukovych fled, and Obama made threats, and Putin moved troops into Crimea, everyone was weighing in, offering opinions, expressing horror, compassion, solidarity. As I pored over "official" news articles shared by "friends" from around the world and "unofficial" reports posted by contacts in Ukraine, Facebook became, for me, a main source of information about the unfolding crisis.[1] But every time I moved the cursor towards my "status line," intent on posting something, *anything*, about what was happening in Ukraine, my fingers froze.

For what it's worth, since I signed up for Facebook I've rarely joined discussions of, or shared links related to, contentious political issues. I use Facebook to share details of my personal life (though even these are carefully chosen and heavily edited), not because I'm politically disengaged but because my "friends" are diverse and I'm averse to conflict, especially when it erupts in the absence of context. I don't want to invite, or involve myself in, online arguments with "friends" or the "friends" of "friends" whose outspokenness will be bolstered by their relative anonymity online. Basically, I'd rather not log on to my Facebook page with knots in my stomach about what I might find, so I keep it simple. I keep it, as much as possible, apolitical.

Oh, but the crisis in Ukraine was different.

It demanded a response from a person like me.

I mean, if you couldn't be *alive* and not have something to say about Ukraine (especially in the early months of 2014, when the crisis made newspaper headlines, again and again, when it was front and centre on television and radio news programs, when it dominated online news sources), then you couldn't be a Ukrainian of any stripe and not have an awful lot to say about it. You certainly couldn't be a scholar whose work has focused on Ukrainian-ness and not offer a responsible response, informed and informative, knowing and knowledgeable. But what would it say about me, a self-avowed Ukrainian Canadian and a scholar, if I inadvertently posted a not altogether credible news story or a biased video clip? What if I delivered an opinion (and it was bound to happen) that overlooked some nuance of the knotted and tangled historical roots of the crisis? Who would I offend (insult, disappoint, embarrass) if I made a statement, however well-intentioned, of "solidarity"? Solidarity with whom, exactly? Those protesting corruption, to be sure, and demanding a say in their country's future. But would solidarity with those critical of Putin imply support for interventions by the United States and other "Western" nations? Would I be reducing what was happening in Ukraine to a narrative of Western good guys fighting to save the passive, helpless damsel – "maidan" – in distress? Even if I could find a way to nuance – historicize and contextualize – my bone-deep sense of solidarity with Ukrainians "on the ground," wouldn't it still come across as flimsy? Surely someone would wonder what solidarity really means when it's fleetingly expressed online by a "Ukrainian" in Canada, during her latté break between trips to Costco and the playground.

On more than one occasion, I have wondered, as I wonder again now, whether anyone really notices what I "say" on Facebook. Regardless, though, of who was or wasn't, is or isn't, paying attention to my Facebook activities, the fact remains that Facebook, like other social networking sites, functions as a form of online "theatre" in which we "perform" our identities. So my "performance anxiety" – let me not mince words, my stage fright – in response to the crisis in Ukraine got me thinking, and thinking deeply, about why I couldn't speak.

I'm speaking now, telling this story here, because doing so throws into sharp relief the anxieties about my Ukrainian-ness that I obviously haven't yet worked out in my writing on the subjects of ethnic and diasporic identities. Marsha Forchuk Skrypuch asks, in the title to her chapter of this book, "Am I Ukrainian?"[2] Since the crisis in Ukraine erupted, I've been asking myself – not for the first time – a slightly different question: "How Ukrainian Am I?" If I can't muster the courage to say something about the crisis. If I'm too busy posting photos of my kid with a face full of *kapusta*. My Facebook story throws into sharp relief, too, the anguished business of being (or trying to be) one of the "poet pedagogues" theorized by Sneja Gunew[3] and discussed by Lindy Ledohowski in her introduction to our collection.[4]

Gunew describes "poet pedagogues" as "artists" who are also "teachers" and who "become the focus for creating and maintaining an intellectual community informed by the diasporic histories of its constituent members and enmeshed in contradictory relations with the dominant cultural paradigms."[5] For a good ten years or so (beginning in 2003, when I published *Kalyna's Song* and finished my PhD), I've thought of myself as a pretty good example of a "poet pedagogue." As recently as weeks ago, when I started rewriting this conclusion, I was quite comfortable positioning myself as a "novelist" and a "scholar," apparently oblivious to the fact that I haven't published any creative writing since my novel was released. Have I aspired to be a "poet pedagogue"? Certainly. My plan, after all, when I started my doctoral studies, was to launch a career as an academic that would subsidize the writing of my novels. While polishing up *Kalyna's Song*, I was writing my dissertation, which would become *Leaving Shadows: Literature in English by Canada's Ukrainians*. Less a labour of love than a means to an end, *Leaving Shadows* was going to get me a job, which was going to make it possible for me to produce more, and better, novels.

Quite apart from the fact that my plan didn't take into account the workload of a full-time professor, I was ill-prepared for the effect on my creative writing that becoming an academic would have. Whatever it was that I did to produce *Kalyna's Song* – and I don't know if I can describe it except to say that I was guided by a character whose motivations I understood and whose story, it seemed to me, needed to be told – I couldn't do now. Having put in ten years as a professional scholar and teacher, I'm governed by a different way of thinking, a different sensibility: call it what you will, it amounts to the same thing. When I've had the time and energy to write creatively, I've found it virtually impossible to turn off or tune out the critic's voice in my head. She's not a monster but she can be monstrous. She has no face, but she has claws, and they're always well-sharpened. All she needs is a whiff of whiteness reinforced as a category of privilege, patriarchy implicitly unchallenged, heteronormativity perpetuated, indigeneity appropriated, nation-building mythologies unquestioned, immigrant experiences idealized, or middle-class subjectivities unproblematized and she's ready to pounce. She's scary, there's no doubt about it, when, ten steps ahead of my most promising ideas for new pieces of creative writing, she anticipates in detail how they will be torn apart by *other* critics, but she's downright terrifying when she dismembers my plans by quoting my own scholarly writing back to me.

Facebook, of course, is a social networking site, not a venue for creative writing, but the fact that I could, and did, work myself into a full-blown neurotic frenzy about saying something about Ukraine on my Facebook page speaks volumes about the power that my "inner critic" wields over me. I would have been far more comfortable "speaking" about Ukraine's crisis on Facebook if I could have posted a forty-page essay in my "status line," complete with explanatory footnotes, pithy quotations drawn from the work of well-respected historians, political scientists, and experts on Ukraine and Eastern Europe, and an extensive bibliography. I probably still would have concluded that I don't understand what's happening in Ukraine, but I would have felt safer drawing even an ambivalent conclusion if, before doing so, I could have demonstrated that I'd done my homework.

You see, scholarly writing, for me, has been a relatively safe space: it's not an uncreative, and definitely not an easy, space to occupy, but it offers protection. To write creatively is to strip down to your bare skin – to give up the armour, not to mention the ammunition, that comes with the conventions of traditional scholarly writing. Scholarly arguments can be bold; often they're contentious; and, increasingly, as academics move towards positioning themselves in relation to their work, they're not impersonal. But the gulf between creative and critical writing remains enormous: the latter, at least for me, just doesn't engender the same vulnerabilities, or involve the same risks, as the former. If my scholarship is questioned, it's my argument that's flawed and/or my research that's incomplete. With nothing between my creative work and me, criticisms of the former feel like attacks on the latter.

This explains, I think, why unflattering reviews of *Leaving Shadows* were far easier for me to slough off than criticisms of *Kalyna's Song*.

It explains why, for the past decade or so, I've chosen to work as a "pedagogue," not a "poet."

When we sent out our call for responses to the question of what it means to be a Ukrainian Canadian "poet pedagogue," we said we would accept essays, poetry, and fictional prose, but we encouraged the writers to hybridize their autobiographical pieces by drawing on the conventions of multiple genres, "creative" and "critical." If I'd been in their shoes, accepting the call would have been tantamount to getting naked while my "inner critic" paced beside me, getting ready to move in for the kill. I wouldn't have had the guts to produce the kind of introspective, self-revelatory writing that the contributors to this volume have delivered via chapters that are at once personal and political, playful and painful, poignant and provocative.

About seven years ago, I started a project with the purpose of reflecting on precisely the kinds of questions raised by this book – questions about the reciprocal relationship between ethnicity and writing, how a writer's ethnic identity simultaneously shapes and is shaped by her work. I was going to make a film documenting my "return" (for the first time) to Ukraine. As a "poet" and a "pedagogue," I planned to make public my personal journey to the "Old Country" by merging the creative and the critical, the theoretical and the experiential. I thought that I would mainly focus on meetings with family members, though I envisioned plenty of footage of me making my way through the streets of Kyiv, Chernivtsi, and Szypentsi ("The Village," from which my maternal and paternal great-grandparents emigrated near the turn of the twentieth century) as, in voice-overs, I textured the "story" of my journey with scholarly analyses of its significance. Early on in the film, I intended to make an homage to Ukrainian Canadian artists and writers – Myrna Kostash, Marusya Bociurkiw, and John Paskievich, especially – who had made and documented similar trips before me and whose work I enormously admired. I was going to position myself as their self-proclaimed acolyte keen on replicating (or mimicking, as best I could) their journeys and discovering what the "new," post-Soviet Ukraine would mean to me, a representative of a "new" generation. My plan was to begin with a quotation from Kostash's *All of Baba's Great Grandchildren: Ethnic Identity in the Next Canada* that seemed to give my project its *raison d'être*: "Each new generation of Canadians," she argues, "has to think through its own relationship to the past and to its own civic desires" because questions about "who we 'really' are" are "never resolved by any particular generation once and for all."[6] In academic terms, my objective was to marry auto/biographical narrative with politicized self-reflexivity, informed by historical analysis and critical theory. In plain language? I wanted to find out if Ukraine felt at all like "home"; and while I suspected that it wouldn't, it seemed possible to me that, in the process of making the film, I could be proven wrong.

Conclusion: Ukrainian Identities On(the)Line 127

The build-up to my journey was, in many ways, exciting and empowering, especially after I secured a research grant to help fund the project and began collaborating with a local cinematographer, Jiri, originally from the Czech Republic, whose diasporic world view seemed well-matched to my own. But as the abstract idea of going to Ukraine became real, I got cold feet. When, in 2009, it came time to book flights, organize accommodation, chart out a detailed itinerary, I started having sleepless nights as I worried about the logistics of the trip and panicked about having a camera thrust in my face, recording my every move, while I struggled to get around and communicate. After one such sleepless night, and a long conversation with my then-boyfriend (now-husband) Mike, I decided that *two* trips would make far better sense than one. Before travelling to Ukraine with Jiri and his gear, I'd first go on a "scouting" mission with Mike, who, despite having no Ukrainians in his family tree, was curious enough about the country to agree to come along. In hindsight, my revised plan should have been my first indication that the project was going sideways. Since the goal was to record my spontaneous experiences and impressions of Ukraine on my first trip "home," the "scouting" trip would fundamentally change, if not undermine altogether, the film's objectives. I didn't care. The idea of doing a practice run with Mike, *sans* cameras, brought me such immense relief that it felt to me, at the time, like a stroke of sheer genius.

So we went, Mike and me. Our plan was to spend two weeks in Ukraine, primarily in Kyiv and Chernivtsi, before taking a train to Istanbul and staying in Turkey for three more weeks. Turkey would be a vacation, plain and simple, but our time in Ukraine would be devoted to film-related work (we'd make preliminary contact with family members, figure out how best to get around with Jiri, and generally get a sense of the "lay of the land"). In the annals of family history, the trip will always have a prominent place because, near the end of it, Mike proposed, on a beach outside of Marmaris. It makes for a good story, how he sweated and fretted every time we crossed a border, worrying that our bags might be searched and the ring discovered; how I resisted joining him on the beach because of the malevolent goats that were grazing nearby.

Many colourful stories came out of that trip, especially the Ukraine portion of it, and I told them a few times, usually to listeners who had no experience and limited knowledge of Ukraine. *Employees smoking at passport-control in the Kyiv airport! Vodka cheaper than coffee! Cars parked every-which-way on sidewalks!* One intuits, I think, or learns fairly quickly, which travel stories will elicit the sought-after responses. In the case of our trip, the self-deprecating stories that I most often chose to tell have been met, as I hoped that they would be, with wide eyes, dropped jaws, and, ultimately, belly laughs.

Looking back now on the Ukraine stories I've told, a pattern forms, one in which both Mike and I struggle with language barriers and culture shock and I alone emerge as at least partly triumphant. On our overnight train trip from Kyiv to Chernivtsi, as we were invited to share *horilka, kolbasa, salo,* and cheese with a couple of guys, roughly our age, whose English was about as appalling as my Ukrainian, *I* was the one who surprised and delighted them with a *"dyakuyu"* and a *"Nazdorovya." I* was the one whose Ukrainian vastly improved as the night wore on. Indeed, were it not for *my* hearty Slavic genes, I might have passed out early, as Mike did, and missed all the cross-cultural fun. Of course, as I discovered the next morning, my Ukrainian language skills no longer dazzled once the liquor left my system: it seems unlikely that they were anything more than a figment of my drunken imagination. And it's equally unlikely likely that I "out-drank" Mike. He was being poured heftier shots, I'm sure, by the Ukrainian guys, one of whom declared his love for me before the night was through.

In a telling commentary on his easy-going nature, Mike wasn't bothered by the Ukrainian guy's advances on me, just as he hasn't been bothered by the stories of our trip that I tell. It bothers me, though, that I've twisted, slanted, and withheld the truth. While it was the case, for example, as Mike and I predicted before we set out, that my Ukrainian language skills were better than his, they were only marginally better (very marginally), and virtually useless when, coupled with my paralysing self-consciousness, I was too ashamed to use them. Because Mike had no problem being – looking, sounding, acting like – a tourist, more often than not *he* was the one, not me, who did our communicating. *He*, with not a word of Ukrainian at his fingertips, found ways to get directions when we were lost and needed help. *He* negotiated taxi fares. *He* ordered food in restaurants with Cyrillic-only menus, even if it meant clucking like a chicken or mooing like a cow.

That I could, and did, ask many strangers for help of various kinds during our time in Turkey, with none of the embarrassment that I felt in Ukraine, makes sense to me: I didn't expect to know much about Turkey, outside of what my guidebook told me, and no one, myself included, would expect me to speak the language there. But Kostash is right: "for a Ukrainian Canadian Ukraine is not a country like other countries."[7] Ukraine wasn't supposed to be strange to me, and Ukrainians weren't supposed to be strangers. We were supposed to be kin. Our interactions were supposed to reveal some sort of visceral bond that transcends geographical borders and linguistic divides. Despite my ostensibly ambivalent motivations for making the film and my cynicism (made explicit in *Leaving Shadows*) about diasporic Ukrainians' largely "imagined" sense of belonging to Ukraine, it became clearer and clearer to me that I somehow thought my journey would be different. I wasn't really aiming to find out *if* Ukraine felt like "home," I was expecting, against all odds, to find out that Ukraine *was* home. My family reunion would unfold effortlessly, with emotional connections zip-zapping electrically over many deliciously simple Ukrainian dishes, against a backdrop of blossoming cherry trees. I imagined tears, stories, spontaneous singing, perhaps dancing. Such are the powerfully emotional resonances, I suppose, of words like "The Village" and "The Old Country." They *over*powered my scholarly research, academic caution, and objective reasoning.

There were no instant, magic connections to be found, though I did experience, throughout the journey, zip-zaps of familiarity that gave me shivers or put a lump in my throat. If I didn't know better, the countryside south of Chernivtsi might have been the farmland where my people settled in Alberta, northeast of Edmonton. It was astonishingly similar. I ate foods that could have been prepared by my aunts or my mother. Hearing Ukrainian spoken everywhere, by everyone, brought me back to my childhood, to family gatherings at my grandparents' little house in Vegreville. Twenty-odd years ago, when *baba* and *gido* passed away, my parents and their siblings stopped speaking Ukrainian. I didn't realize how much I missed the sounds of Ukrainian – undecipherable to me but comforting, soothing. The sounds of home.

It was painful, reconciling the sounds and tastes and visual reminders of "home" with my conspicuous outsider-ness in my "homeland." I didn't want to feel or look or sound so out of place. But then, what did I expect, decked out in my many-pocketed cargo pants and handwashable/fast-drying T-shirts (guaranteed by Mountain Equipment Co-op to be the ideal travellers' attire), not to mention my hiking shoeboot hybrids (good for walking long distances)? Of course I got funny glances, and a lot of them, from real Ukrainians. Next to the well-dressed women of Kyiv, especially, in their high heels and silky stockings, I must have looked like I'd arrived in a canoe. People stared, and

I met their stares with the big, goofy grins that, I've since been told, are characteristically Canadian, not Ukrainian. I didn't have to open my mouth and let loose a single syllable of badly pronounced, babyish Ukrainian for any local to see me for what I was: a tourist.

In the end, there would be no film. There wasn't much of a story to be told. Even the colourful anecdotes about the trip that I used to trot out feel to me, now, clichéd, so I've retired them. Everyone who has been to Ukraine has a train story.

I took it as a sign when, two or three years after Mike and I returned to Canada, all of our Ukraine photos and videos melted down in a collapse of my computer's hard drive. It says something, I think, that I never backed up those Ukraine-files and that I hardly blinked an eye when they were lost. Aside from our memories, the stories we choose to tell, and a "slide show" of pictures that I posted on (where else?) Facebook, we have nothing to prove that our trip ever happened.

So I come full circle, I suppose, back to my anxieties about commenting online about the crisis in Ukraine, and back to my "inner critic," who started to find her voice somewhere over the Atlantic, as Mike and I chatted about wedding plans and I began a list of reasons for abandoning the film project.

What I take away from it all directly relates to *this* project – which, in academic terms, foregrounds the dynamic and diverse ways in which contemporary Canadian writers of Ukrainian origin continually renegotiate and reconstruct the meaning of their identities, communities, and histories (all plural, all interrelated, none fixed).

In plain language?

The writers who have contributed to this collection have guts. (I don't strictly mean the guts it takes to travel repeatedly to Ukraine, as many of them have, and then to write – and, in Marusya Bociurkiw's case, also make stunning films – about their experiences, though it most certainly is not lost on me that Myrna Kostash, Erín Moure, Marusya Bociurkiw, and Janice Kulyk Keefer have shown that they have what it takes to do so.) They take risks, again and again. (Despite, for example, the low "tolerance" for "an ethnic presence" in works of commercial fiction, not to mention her fears that Ukrainian readers would balk at the "profanity" and "explicit scenes" that appear in *The Prairie Bridesmaid*,[8] Daria Salamon decided to foreground her protagonist's Ukrainian-ness *and* leave in the lesbian sex.) They break new ground, break rules, break with tradition. They are unbound. They break down borders. (I think here about the collapsing of the "borders" between poetry and prose in

"Tuteshni," and how it mirrors Moure's sense of belonging not to the geopolitically demarcated nation-state of Ukraine but to the "borderland" described by her mother as *"nowhere."* I think about the ways in which the poems collected in *The Unmemntioable* serve to dissolve the emotional "borders" between grief and joy so that Moure finds herself able to "mourn, and admit, and rejoice, and mourn, and embrace, and be present with [her] Ukrainian and Galician friends," honouring "what remains and what was lost, alongside them."[9]) They bend genres but they don't bend to the expectations of "the" Ukrainian Canadian community. They keep writing ("constantly," as Bociurkiw describes it, "obsessively"[10]) about their experiences of ethnic identity and community, even when they're taken to task for what they write, sometimes by the people closest to them (Skrypuch talks about how "downright frightening" some of her readers' responses to her Ukrainian-themed books have been,[11] and Bociurkiw alludes to being disowned by her *baba*, "the love of [her] life," because of her work[12]). They don't give in and they don't give up. If they, too, are hounded by the voices of "inner critics," they've found a way to put those critics' voices to good use by effortlessly merging the "creative" and the "critical."

They make it *seem* effortless, I should say: in reality, the work they produce and the sacrifices they make to produce it require more effort that most of us can imagine, must less muster. Yet they keep narrating, with confidence, the "in between" spaces that they – all of them – occupy. Elizabeth Bachinsky admits to not knowing "very much about what it meant to be a part of a Ukrainian Canadian community";[13] Moure inherits from her mother the sense of being from *"nowhere"*;[14] Bociurkiw is alienated from her family by her mother's and *baba's* shame; Skrypuch explicitly notes that it is "not the sense of being Ukrainian that resonates most deeply" for her but, rather, the "sense of not belonging";[15] and Kostash, in her identification with all of those, but especially her "Doomed Bridegrooms," who have been "exiled to the margins of the dominant narratives of Western Christian, Enlightenment, and Imperial cultures," expresses her sense of herself as an outsider.[16] Readers of this book cannot miss the fact that virtually every contributor mentions, in one way or another, her feeling of un-belonging. At the same time, in the work collected here there is as much hope and optimism as there is grief and pain. Bociurkiw reconciles with her mother over food and stories at an unlikely gathering of the "Divas of the Church" and a "gang of dykes from the university."[17] Even if Salamon continues to be scolded by her *baba* for not speaking

Ukrainian "properly" and "pestered" by her mother for not regularly going to church, her book is warmly received by readers, Ukrainian Canadians and non–Ukrainian Canadians alike.[18] And although Ukrainian Canadians' acceptance of Skrypuch's Ukrainian-themed writing has been hard-won, "various Armenian groups" immediately "opened their arms" to her, in response to her Armenian-themed books, making her "feel welcome"[19] and suggesting that what Kulyk Keefer concludes about her own "betwixt and between" identity[20] is probably true for Skrypuch as well. It may well be true for all of us that the community in which we feel most "at home" is one "composed not of any one ethnic or linguistic group, but of all those who are stranded between languages, or struggling to make peace with the demands of different cultures."[21]

The contributors to this book look inward and outward, at themselves and towards their readers, reminding us all that we're not alone: we *are* a community, we who live between languages, between cultures, between worlds. They show us that, whether it's via commercial fiction, children's literature, poetry, creative non-fiction, literary fiction, academic writing, or filmmaking, we speak in equally valid ways. And, as importantly, they remind us that our silences (a line from Elizabeth Bachinsky's chapter – "I can't begin to write / about this" – has helped me come to terms with my inability to speak about the crisis in Ukraine)[22] can be as powerful as our speech.

I can't predict what this book will become once it "goes out into the world" but I believe that Bociurkiw is right: it will come back, "many months" from now, "a different book."[23] I hope that readers, too, will be changed for having read it, as I've been changed by working on it. I'm talking about small changes, modest shifts: recognizing that much work remains to be done to address the tendencies for Ukrainian Canadian literature to fall through the cracks of Canadian and diasporic literary studies. We need scholars' dogged commitment to drawing attention to the vibrant voices of "Ukrainian Canada" – in our journal articles, in our monographs, in our edited collections, in our book reviews – to correct the sheer wrongness of what Myrna Kostash, speaking about her own writing (though she could as well be describing the writing of the other "poet pedagogues" included in this book), refers to as a body of work "marginalized, unstudied, and unacknowledged, and subject to the communities' taboos, whether of ethnicity, gender, location, or ideology."[24] Perhaps most importantly, we need *pedagogues'* fierce dedication to bringing the work of Ukrainian Canadian writers to the captive audiences of our classrooms: to the hundreds of students who demonstrate, term after term, year after year, how captiv*ating* – politically awakening, emotionally evocative, aesthetically eye-opening – the voices of Ukrainian Canada can be. What I sought to accomplish with my film has been, and is, accomplished many times over through the transformative conversations I have had, and continue to have, with my students about the relation between writing, identity, community, and history. These conversations couldn't and wouldn't happen if I were oblivious to the fact that my work as a pedagogue is "poetic" (effective teaching requires creativity, and a full mobilization of the imagination) and performative. Every class I teach *is* a performance: it's a one-woman show and, at the same time, interactive theatre; it's scripted and improvised; it's personal and political, playful and painful, poignant and provocative. In institutional settings, which, despite the interventions of feminist, queer, and postcolonial scholars, still tend to privilege canonical texts, it's a risk to include Ukrainian Canadian/feminist/leftist/queer writers on a reading list. It takes guts to teach the work of the writers who are included in this book, and the work of writers like them.

A lifetime ago, or so it seems, in *Leaving Shadows*, I urged readers to "*write [their] stories down; make [their] voices heard*".[25] I don't know if, today, I see completely eye-to-eye with the person who wrote those words. I still believe that we all have stories to tell: of course we do. I believe, too, that we're all storytellers. But I'm not sure that we're all writers. Or maybe we're writers for a while, and then we're teachers, or filmmakers, or mothers, or academics. Some of us do, or will, find a way to be all of these; some of us don't, and won't. None of us, though, will be lesser for the choices we make, and it seems to me important for us to remind ourselves that we're not tethered to these choices. We really do "renegotiate and reconstruct" our identities, continually. Who we are, today; what we say, in this moment, about our "selves" and our histories; the parts that we play in our unbound "betwixt and between"[26] community – these are all necessarily provisional: subject to change, open to revision. In this, we have something vaguely in common, I suspect, with the people of Ukraine, despite the geographical, cultural, social, and political distances between us.

I suspect, too, that I will write creatively again, though maybe not until we send our kid "out in the world."[27] In the meantime, I vacillate between wanting to fast-forward the story of her life, because I can't wait to find out who and what she will be, and wishing that I could slow the clock and the calendar, so that she'll remain just as she is now: "Our Little Ukrainian Girl," devouring *baba's holuptsi*, staring into my dad's eyes as they dance an old time waltz around our living room, asking for "mo' pease" ("more please") after I've finished singing her one of the Ukrainian folk songs that my mother taught me. Do I worry that I'm giving her fragments and remnants of a rich and vibrant culture, superficial bits and pieces of food and song and dance disconnected from both the fraught, complex history of Ukraine and the equally fraught, complex unfolding of that country's future? I do. Constantly. I worry that a day will come when she becomes indifferent even to these bits and pieces, questioning (or, worse, rejecting outright) the ethnic label that I affixed to her on Facebook. Truth be told, I'm not convinced that she has a fighting chance at growing up "Ukrainian." When she asks what the words of the folk songs mean, I won't be able to tell her. I won't be able to enrol her in a Ukrainian immersion program or bilingual school because none exists in our area. I'm not part of the small Ukrainian Canadian community in the Okanagan or a member of the few Ukrainian churches that provide services for them.

Yes. It seems unlikely that my little girl, with her unmistakably French first and last names, will wind up "Ukrainian."

Then again, my voice is just one of many that she will hear and read as she grows up. The contributors who fill this volume also fill my bookshelves. Some of them – like Kulyk Keefer (who describes her sons' "unhyphenated" Canadian identities as a motivating factor in her decision to begin writing about her ethnicity),[28] Skrypuch, Salamon, and Bachinsky (whose daughter was born as we put this book together) – are mothers themselves; others are "expecting" or contemplating adoption. Or they have decided, as Kostash phrases it in *The Doomed Bridegroom*, to *"bear books."*[29] Collectively, if I have anything to say about it, these writers will show Esmé that ethnicity is experienced and expressed in multiple ways, just as they have shown me that "maternal" legacies are as varied as they are valid. And if I really believe in what they've taught me about the provisional nature of our identities, the ways in which our "selves" shift and change, then I have to not only accept who I am right now, in our age of social media – a typical middle-class mother with a computer who's going to keep putting up photos of her daughter on Facebook – but also allow for the possibility that who she and I both become might just surprise us all.

NOTES

1. Facebook and Twitter have played an integral role in the dissemination of information related to the crisis in Ukraine since the first protests began. They were indispensable to activists and demonstrators, who in early 2011 began using these social networking sites to organize protests and raise awareness of the "Arab Spring" demonstrations.
2. Skrypuch, "Am I Ukrainian?," 65.
3. Gunew, *Haunted Nations*, 13.
4. Ledohowski, "Ukrainian Canadian Poet Pedagogues," 4.
5. Gunew, *Haunted Nations*, 13.
6. Kostash, *All of Baba's Great-Grandchildren*, 37.
7. Kostash, *Bloodlines*, 168.
8. Salamon, "Putting the *Baba* Back in the Book," 102, 107.
9. Moure, "Tuteshni," 91.
10. Bociurkiw, "Bringing Back Memory," 75.
11. Skrypuch, "Am I Ukrainian?," 71.
12. Bociurkiw, "Bringing Back Memory," 74.
13. Bachinsky, "Eight Things," 42.
14. Moure, "Tuteshni," 91.
15. Skrypuch, "Am I Ukrainian?," 65.
16. Kostash, "The Gulag, the Crypt, and the Gallows," 110.
17. Bociurkiw, "Bringing Back Memory," 79.
18. Salamon, "Putting the *Baba* Back in the Book," 108.
19. Skrypuch, "Am I Ukrainian?," 71.
20. Kulyk Keefer, "Language Lessons," 23.
21. Ibid., 39.
22. Bachinsky, "Eight Things," 52.
23. Bociurkiw, "Bringing Back Memory," 78.
24. Kostash, "The Gulag, the Crypt, and the Gallows," 119.
25. Grekul, *Leaving Shadows*, xxiii.
26. Kulyk Keefer, "Language Lessons," 23.
27. Bociurkiw, "Bringing Back Memory," 78.
28. Kulyk Keefer, "Coming across Bones," 89.
29. Kostash, *The Doomed Bridegroom*, 54.

Appendix

Bibliography of English-Language Ukrainian Canadian Literature, 1954–2009: 55 Years of English-Language Ukrainian Canadian Writing

The following list of creative literature written by and about Ukrainian Canadians will be of interest to students, teachers, readers, and writers of all varieties. It offers readers interested in this material a resource, a starting point for the many textual conversations and interventions in the ongoing development of Ukrainian Canadian-ness. The criteria used to determine inclusion in this list is straightforward: simply that the author has been identified as Ukrainian Canadian in some way and that the text itself foregrounds questions about this particular ethnocultural identity. Gayatri Chakravorty Spivak famously referred to the "native informant" as she or he who writes from within a supposedly coherent group for an external audience eager for "authentic" representation.[1] This entire manuscript, including the appendix, questions this very notion of coherence while simultaneously trading on this desire to find "authentic" voices.

Anthologies

Balan, Jars, ed. *Prairie Fire* 13, no. 3, 1992.
Balan, Jars, and Yuri Klynovy, eds. *Yarmarok: Ukrainian Writing in Canada Since the Second World War*. Edmonton: CIUS, University of Alberta, 1987.
Kulyk Keefer, Janice, and Solomea Pavlychko, eds. *Two Lands New Visions: Stories from Canada and Ukraine*. Regina: Coteau Books, 1999.
Skrypuch, Marsha Forchuk, ed. *Kobzar's Children: A Century of Untold Ukrainian Stories*. Markham: Fitzhenry and Whiteside, 2006.

Fiction

Bereshko, Ludmilla [Fran Ponomarenko]. *The Parcel from Chicken Street and Other Stories*. Montreal: DC Books, 1989.

Appendix

Bociurkiw, Marusya. *The Children of Mary*. Toronto: Inanna, 2006.
– *The Woman Who Loved Airports*. Vancouver: Press Gang, 1994.
Borsky, Mary. *Influence of the Moon*. Erin: Porcupine's Quill, 2008.
Dawydiak, Orysia. *House of Bears*. Woodstock: Acorn Books, 2009.
Evanishen, Danny. *Vuiko Yurko: The First Generation*. Summerland: Ethnic Enterprises, Publishing Division, 1994.
– *Vuiko Yurko: Second-Hand Stories*. Summerland: Ethnic Enterprises, Publishing Division, 1997.
Grekul, Lisa. *Kalyna's Song*. Regina: Coteau Books, 2003. [also marketed as young adult fiction]
Haas, Maara. *On Stage with Maara Haas*. Winnipeg: Lilith Publications, 1986.
– *The Street Where I Live*. Toronto: McGraw-Hill Ryerson, 1976.
Hawrelak, Nancy. *Breaking Ground*. Vegreville: Willow Press, 1998.
Kulyk Keefer, Janice. *The Green Library*. Toronto: HarperCollins, 1996.
– *The Ladies' Lending Library*. Toronto: HarperCollins, 2007.
Kupchenko, Yuri. *The Horseman of Shandro Crossing*. Edmonton: Tree Frog Press, 1989.
Kupchenko Frolick, Gloria. *The Chicken Man*. Stratford: William-Wallace Publishers, 1989.
– *The Green Tomato Years*. Toronto: William-Wallace Publishers, 1985.
Lysenko, Vera. *Westerly Wild*. Toronto: The Ryerson Press, 1956.
– *Yellow Boots*. 1954. Edmonton: CIUS and NeWest Press, 1992.
Mitchell, Shandi. *Under This Unbroken Sky*. Toronto: Penguin, 2009.
Potrebenko, Helen. *Hey Waitress and Other Stories*. Vancouver: Lazara Press, 1989.
Rosnau, Laisha. *The Sudden Weight of Snow*. Toronto: McClelland and Stewart, 2002.
Ryga, George. "Ballad of a Stonepicker" (1976). In *George Ryga: The Prairie Novels*, edited by James Hoffman. 139–234. Vancouver: Talonbooks, 2004.
– "Hungry Hills" (1974). In *George Ryga: The Prairie Novels*, edited by James Hoffman. 21–37. Vancouver: Talonbooks, 2004.
– "Night Desk" (1976). In *George Ryga: The Prairie Novels*, edited by James Hoffman. 235–316.Vancouver: Talonbooks, 2004.
Salamon, Daria. *The Prairie Bridesmaid*. Toronto: Key Porter Books, 2008.
Slobodian, Sophia. *The Glistening Furrow*. Edmonton: Reidmore Books, 1983.
– *Let the Soft Wind Blow*. Edmonton: Reidmore Books, 1993.
Talpash, Orest S. *Rybalski's Son*. Victoria: Trafford Publishing, 2008.
Warring, Molly Anne. *Paradise Acres: The Stry-Ker Family Saga*. Ottawa: Borealis Press, 2006.
Warwaruk, Larry. *Ukrainian Wedding*. Regina: Coteau Books, 1998.

Children's/Young Adult Fiction

Borsky, Mary. *Benny Bensky and the Giant Pumpkin Heist*. Toronto: Tundra Books, 2002.
– *Benny Bensky and the Parrot-Napper*. Toronto: Tundra Books, 2008.
– *Benny Bensky and the Perogy Palace*. Toronto: Tundra Books, 2001.
Goldstone, Gabriele. *The Kulak's Daughter*. Austin: Blooming Tree Press, 2009.
Grekul, Lisa. *Kalyna's Song*. Regina: Coteau Books, 2003. [also marketed as mainstream fiction]
Kupchenko Frolick, Gloria. *Anna Veryha*. Toronto: Maxwell Macmillan, 1994.
Langston, Laura. *Lesia's Dream*. Toronto: HarperCollins Children's Books, 2003.
Skrypuch, Marsha Forchuk. *Dear Canada: Prisoners in the Promised Land*. Toronto: Scholastic Canada, 2007.
– *Hope's War*. Toronto: A Boardwalk Book, 2001.
– *Silver Threads*. 1996. Markham: Fitzhenry and Whiteside, 2004.
– *Stolen Child*. Toronto: Scholastic Canada, 2010.
Warwaruk, Larry. *Andrei and the Snow Walker*. Regina: Coteau Books, 2002.

Poetry

Bachinsky, Elizabeth. *God of Missed Connections*. Gibsons: Nightwood Editions, 2009.
Bociurkiw, Marusya. *Halfway to the East*. Vancouver: Lazara Press, 1999.
Kulyk Keefer, Janice. *Midnight Stroll*. Holstein: Exile Editions, 2006.
– *Burden of Innocence / Foreign Relations*. Rodovid, 2009.
Suknaski, Andrew. *In the Name of Narid*, edited by Dennis Cooley. Erin Mills: Porcupine's Quill, 1981.
– *Wood Mountain Poems*, edited by Al Purdy. Toronto: Macmillan, 1976.

Drama

Galay, Ted. *After Baba's Funeral and Sweet and Sour Pickles*. Toronto: Playwrights Canada Press, 1981.
Ryga, George. "A Letter to My Son." *A Portrait of Angelica – A Letter to My Son*. Winnipeg: Turnstone Press, 1984. 69–117.
Schur, Danny, and Rick Chafe. *Strike!* Toronto: Playwrights Canada Press, 2005.

Memoir / Creative Non-Fiction

Bociurkiw, Marusya. *Comfort Food for Breakups: The Memoir of a Hungry Girl.* Vancouver: Arsenal Pulp Press, 2007.

Dedora, Brian. *With WK in the Workshop: A Memoir of William Kurelek.* Stratford: Aya Press / Mercury Press, 1989.

Fodchuk, Roman. *ZHORNA: Material Culture of the Ukrainian Pioneers.* Calgary: University of Calgary Press, 2006.

Gerus, Oleh W., and Denis Hlynka, eds. *The Honourable Member for Vegreville: The Memoirs and Diary of Anthony Hlynka, MP.* Calgary: University of Calgary Press, 2005.

Kostash, Myrna. *All of Baba's Children.* 1977. Edmonton: NeWest Press, 1987.

– *All of Baba's Great Grandchildren: Ethnic Identity in the Next Canada.* Saskatoon: Heritage, 2000.

– *Bloodlines: A Journey into Eastern Europe.* Vancouver: Douglas and McIntyre, 1993.

– *The Doomed Bridegroom: A Memoir.* Edmonton: NeWest Publishers, 1998.

Kulyk Keefer, Janice. *Honey and Ashes: A Story of Family.* Toronto: HarperCollins, 1998.

– *Dark Ghost in the Corner: Imagining Ukrainian-Canadian Identity.* Saskatoon: Heritage Press, 2005.

Potrebenko, Helen. *No Streets of Gold: A Social History of Ukrainians in Alberta.* Vancouver: New Star Books, 1977.

Radchuk, Serge. *I Chose Canada, A Memoir.* Steinbach: Derksen Printers, 2001.

NOTE

1 Spivak, "Can the Subaltern Speak?"

References

Bachinsky, Elizabeth. "Eight Things." In *Unbound: Ukrainian Canadians Writing Home*, edited by Lisa Grekul and Lindy Ledohowski. 41–64. Toronto: University of Toronto Press, 2016.
– *God of Missed Connections*. Gibsons: Nightwood Editions, 2009.
Balan, Jars. "Introduction: 'One Anthology – Two Literatures.'" In *Yarmarok: Ukrainian Writing in Canada Since the Second World War*, edited by Jars Balan and Yuri Klynovy. xv–xix. Edmonton: CIUS, University of Alberta Press, 1987.
– *Salt and Braided Bread: Ukrainian Life in Canada*. Toronto: Oxford University Press, 1984.
– ed. *Identifications: Ethnicity and the Writer in Canada*. Edmonton: CIUS, University of Alberta Press, 1982.
Batuman, Elif. "Get a Real Degree." *London Review of Books* 32, no. 18 (2010): 3–8.
Benjamin, Walter. "The Work of Art in the Age of Mechanical Reproduction." In *Illuminations*, edited by Hannah Arendt, translated by Harry Zohn [from the 1935 essay]. 217–52. New York: Schocken Books, 1969.
Bociurkiw, Marusya. "Bordercrossings: Skin/Voice/Identity." *Canadian Woman Studies / les cahiers de la femme* 14, no. 1 (1993): 6–8.
– "Bringing Back Memory." In *Unbound: Ukrainian Canadians Writing Home*, edited by Lisa Grekul and Lindy Ledohowski. 73–85. Toronto: University of Toronto Press, 2016.
– *The Children of Mary*. Toronto: Inanna, 2006.
– *Comfort Food for Breakups: The Memoir of a Hungry Girl*. Vancouver: Arsenal Pulp Press, 2007.
Bychinsky, Anna Kuryla. "The Dowry." *Maclean's*, 1 February 1926, 13–14, 53–6.

- "Zonia's Revolt." *Maclean's*, 15 April 1924, 14–15, 60–5.
Chamberlain, William Henry. *The Ukraine: A Submerged Nation*. New York: Macmillan, 1944.
Darwent, Charles. "Arrows of Desire: How Did St. Sebastian Become an Enduring, Homo-Erotic Icon?" *The Independent*, 10 February 2008. Accessed 5 March 2015. http://www.independent.co.uk/arts-entertainment/art/features/arrows-of-desire-how-did-st-sebastian-become-an-enduring-homoerotic-icon-779388.html?action=Gallery&ino=7.
Dixon, Jennifer M. "Defending the Nation? Maintaining Turkey's Narrative of the Armenian Genocide." *South European Society and Politics* 15, no. 3 (2010): 467–85.
Doucet, Clive. *Notes from Exile: On Being Acadian*. Toronto: McClelland and Stewart, 2000.
Edelson, Miriam. "Letting Go of the Union Label: The Feminization of a Macho Myth." *The Magazine* (October–November 1991): n.p.
Epp, Marlene, Franca Iacovetta, and Frances Swyripa, eds. *Sisters or Strangers? Immigrant, Ethnic, and Racialized Women in Canadian History*. Toronto: University of Toronto Press, 2004.
Ewanchuk, Michael. *Pioneer Profiles: Ukrainian Settlers in Manitoba*. Winnipeg: Derksen Printer and M. Ewanchuk, 1981.
Fee, Margery, Sneja Gunew, and Lisa Grekul. "Myrna Kostash: Ukrainian Canadian Non-Fiction Prairie New Leftist Feminist Canadian Nationalist." *Canadian Literature* 172 (2002): 114–43.
Grekul, Lisa. *Leaving Shadows: Literature in English by Canada's Ukrainians*. Edmonton: University of Alberta Press, 2005.
- "Re-placing Ethnicity: Literature in English by Canada's Ukrainians." PhD diss., University of British Columbia, 2003.
- "Re-placing Ethnicity: New Approaches to Ukrainian Canadian Literature." In *Home-Work: Postcolonialism, Pedagogy, and Canadian Literature*, edited by Cynthia Sugars. 369–83. Ottawa: University of Ottawa Press, 2004.
Gunew, Sneja. *Haunted Nations: The Colonial Dimensions of Multiculturalisms*. New York: Routledge, 2004.
Harrington, Walt. "The Writer's Choice: Truth May Be Many Things, But It Is Not Nothing." *Newsletter of the IALJS* 2, no. 1 (2008): 11.
Hlynka, Isydore. *The Other Canadians: Selected Articles from the Column of "Ivan Harmata" Published in the* Ukrainian Voice. Winnipeg: Trident Press, 1981.
Hryniuk, Stella, and Lubomyr Luciuk, eds. *Canada's Ukrainians: Negotiating an Identity*. Toronto: Multicultural Society of Ontario, 1993.
James-Dunbar, Heidi. "Authenticity and Textual Violence: The Case for Autofiction." *Open Democracy*, 6 April 2010. Accessed 5 March

2015. https://www.opendemocracy.net/heidi-james-dunbar/authenticity-and-textual-violence-case-for-autofiction.

Kamboureli, Smaro. "Introduction." In *Making a Difference: Canadian Multicultural Literature*, edited by Smaro Kamboureli. 1–16. Toronto: Oxford University Press, 1996.

Kirkconnell, Watson. Review of *Yellow Boots* by Vera Lysenko. *University of Toronto Quarterly* 17 (1947): 425–9.

Kirtz, Mary. "Old World Traditions, New World Inventions: Bilingualism, Multiculturalism, and the Transformation of Ethnicity." *Canadian Ethnic Studies* 28, no. 1 (1996): 8–21.

Klymasz, Robert. Review of *Prairie Fire: A Canadian Magazine of New Writing 13, no. 3: Echoes from Ukrainian Canada*. *Canadian Ethnic Studies* 26, no. 1 (1994): 163–4.

Kolasky, John. *Education in Soviet Ukraine: A Study in Discrimination and Russification*. Toronto: Peter Martin, 1968.

Kordan, Bohdan. *Enemy Aliens: Prisoners of War: Internment in Canada during the Great War*. Montreal and Kingston: McGill-Queen's University Press, 2002.

Kordan, Bohdan, and Craig Mahovsky. *A Bare and Impolitic Right: Internment and Ukrainian Canadian Redress*. Montreal and Kingston: McGill-Queen's University Press, 2004.

Kordan, Bohdan, and Peter Melnycky. *In the Shadow of the Rockies: Diary of the Castle Mountain Internment Camp*. Edmonton: CIUS Press, 1991.

Kostash, Myrna. *All of Baba's Children*. 1977. Edmonton: NeWest Press, 1987.

– *All of Baba's Great Grandchildren*. Saskatoon: Heritage Press, 2000.

– *Bloodlines: A Journey Into Eastern Europe*. Vancouver: Douglas and McIntyre, 1993.

– *The Doomed Bridegroom: A Memoir*. Edmonton: NeWest Press, 1998.

– "The Gulag, the Crypt, and the Gallows: Sites of Ukrainian Canadian Desire." In *Unbound: Ukrainian Canadians Writing Home*, edited by Lisa Grekul and Lindy Ledohowski. 109–20. Toronto: University of Toronto Press, 2016.

– "Inside the Copper Mountain." In *Why Are You Telling Me This? Eleven Acts of Intimate Journalism*, edited by Heather Elton, Barbara Moon, and Don Obe. 89–120. Banff: Banff Centre Press, 1997.

– "The Shock of White Cognition." *Border Crossings* 13, no. 3 (1994): 4–5.

– "Writers Read; Readers Write: Democratising the Relationship." In *Driving Home: A Dialogue between Writers and Readers*, edited by Barbara Belyea. 61–5. Waterloo: Wilfrid Laurier University Press, 1984.

Kulyk Keefer, Janice. "Coming Across Bones: Historiographic Ethnofiction." *Essays on Canadian Writing* 57 (1995): 84–104.

- *Dark Ghost in the Corner: Imagining Ukrainian Canadian Identity.* Saskatoon: Heritage Press, 2005.
- "Language Lessons." In *Unbound: Ukrainian Canadians Writing Home*, edited by Lisa Grekul and Lindy Ledohowski. 23–40. Toronto: University of Toronto Press, 2016.

Ledohowski, Lindy. "Becoming the Hyphen: The Evolution of English-Language Ukrainian Canadian Literature." *Canadian Ethnic Studies / études ethniques au Canada* 39, no. 1–2 (2007): 107–27.
- "Canadian Cossacks: Finding Ukraine in Fifty Years of Ukrainian-Canadian Literature in English." PhD diss., University of Toronto, 2008.
- "'I Am Enchanted': The Home Country as Dead Lover in Myrna Kostash's *The Doomed Bridegroom*." In *Narratives of Citizenship: Indigenous and Diasporic Peoples Unsettle the Nation-State*, edited by Aloys Fleishmann, Nancy VanStyendale, and Cody McCarroll. 129–48. Edmonton: University of Alberta Press, 2011.
- "Little Ukraine on the Prairie: 'Baba' in English-Language Ukrainian-Canadian Literature." In *Place and Replace: Essays on Western Canada*, edited by Adele Perry, Essyllt Jones, and Leah Morton. 186–206. Winnipeg: University of Manitoba Press, 2013.
- "Ukrainian Canadian Poet Pedagogues." In *Unbound: Ukrainian Canadians Writing Home*, edited by Lisa Grekul and Lindy Ledohowski. 3–22. Toronto: University of Toronto Press, 2016.

Lewycka, Marina. *A Short History of Tractors in Ukrainian*. London: Penguin Books, 2006.
- "Ukraine and the West: Hot Air and Hypocrisy." *The Guardian*, 10 March 2014. Accessed 5 March 2015. http://www.theguardian.com/world/2014/mar/10/ukraine-and-west-hot-air-hypocrisy-crimea-russia.

Luciuk, Lubomyr. *Righting an Injustice: The Debate over Redress for Canada's First National Internment Operations*. Toronto: Justinian Press, 1994.
- *Without Just Cause*. Kingston: Kashtan Press, 2006.

Lupul, Manoly. *A Heritage in Transition*. Toronto: McClelland and Stewart, 1982.

Lysenko, Vera. *Men in Sheepskin Coats: A Study in Assimilation*. Toronto: The Ryerson Press, 1947.

MacFarquhar, Larissa. "The Dead Are Real: Hilary Mantel's Imagination." *The New Yorker*, 15 October 2012. Accessed 5 March 2015. http://www.newyorker.com/magazine/2012/10/15/the-dead-are-real.

Mackey, Eva. *The House of Difference: Cultural Politics and National Identity in Canada*. Toronto: University of Toronto Press, 2002.

Manning, Clarence A. *The Story of the Ukraine*. New York: Philosophical Society, 1947.

– *Twentieth-Century Ukraine*. New York: Bookman, 1951.
Martynowych, Orest. *Ukrainians in Canada: The Formative Years, 1891–1924*. Edmonton: CIUS Press, 1991.
Marunchak, Michael. *The Ukrainian Canadians: A History*. Winnipeg: Ukrainian Academy of Arts and Sciences, 1981.
McLean, Elizabeth. "The Siege of Fort Pitt," "Prisoners of the Indians," and "Our Captivity Ended." In *The Frog Lake Massacre: Personal Perspectives on Ethnic Conflict*, edited by Stuart Hughes. 272–95. Toronto: McClelland and Stewart, 1976.
Mitchell, Shandi. *Under This Unbroken Sky*. Toronto: Penguin Canada, 2008.
Moodley, Koglia. "Canadian Multiculturalism as Ideology." *Ethnic and Racial Studies* 6, no. 3 (1983): 321–30.
Moure, Erín. *O Cidadán: Poems*. Toronto: House of Anansi, 2002.
– "Tuteshni." In *Unbound: Ukrainian Canadians Writing Home*, edited by Lisa Grekul and Lindy Ledohowski. 86–99. Toronto: University of Toronto Press, 2016.
– *The Unmemntioable*. Toronto: House of Anansi, 2012.
Mycak, Sonia. *Canuke Literature: Critical Essays on Ukrainian Canadian Writing*. Huntington: Nova Science Publications, 2001.
Nibley, Hugh W. *The Early Christian Prayer Circle*. Accessed 5 March 2015. http://bhporter.com/Nibley%20Early%20Christian%20Prayer%20Circle.htm.
Padolsky, Enoch. "Canadian Ethnic Minority Literature in English." In *Ethnicity and Culture in Canada: The Research Landscape*, edited by J.W. Berry and J.A. Laponce. 361–86. Toronto: University of Toronto Press, 1994.
Paluk, William. *Canadian Cossacks: Essays, Articles, and Stories on Ukrainian Canadian Life*. Winnipeg: Winnipeg Ukrainian Canadian Review, 1943.
Paré, François. *Exiguity: Reflections on the Margins of Literature*. Translated by Lin Burman. Waterloo: Wilfrid Laurier University Press, 1997.
Phillips, Eileen. *The Left and the Erotic*. London: Lawrence and Wishart, 1983.
Porter, John. *The Vertical Mosaic: An Analysis of Social Class and Power in Canada*. Toronto: University of Toronto Press, 1965.
Potrebenko, Helen. Review of *Leaving Shadows: Literature in English by Canada's Ukrainians* by Lisa Grekul. *Canadian Literature* 193 (2007): 99–100.
Pullman, Philip. "Carnegie Medal Acceptance Speech." Accessed 5 March 2015. http://www.randomhouse.com/features/pullman/author/carnegie.php.
Robertson, Patricia. "Marriage à la (Winnipeg) Mode." *Globe and Mail*, 9 August 2008. Accessed 5 March 2015. http://www.theglobeandmail.com/arts/marriage-la-winnipeg-mode/article715455.

Rubchak, Marian J. "Ukraine's Ancient Matriarch as a Topos in Constructing a Feminine Identity." *Feminist Review* 92 (2009): 129–50.

Salamon, Daria. "Putting the *Baba* Back in the Book." In *Unbound: Ukrainian Canadians Writing Home*, edited by Lisa Grekul and Lindy Ledohowski. 100–8. Toronto: University of Toronto Press, 2016.

Skrypuch, Marsha Forchuk. "Am I Ukrainian?" In *Unbound: Ukrainian Canadians Writing Home*, edited by Lisa Grekul and Lindy Ledohowski. 65–72. Toronto: University of Toronto Press, 2016.

– *Hope's War*. Toronto: A Boardwalk Book, 2001.

– *The Hunger*. Toronto: Dundurn, 1999.

– *Making Bombs for Hitler*. Toronto: Scholastic Canada, 2012.

– *Silver Threads*. Toronto: Penguin Canada, 1996.

– *Stolen Child*. Toronto: Scholastic Canada, 2010.

Slemon, Stephen. "Why Do I Have to Write Like That?" *English Studies in Canada* 32, no. 2–3 (2006): 1–3.

Spivak, Gayatri Chakravorty. "Can the Subaltern Speak?" In *Marxism and the Interpretation of Culture*, edited by Cary Nelson and Lawrence Grossberg. 271–313. London: Macmillan, 1988.

Sridharan, Vasudeyan. "Kiev Protests: Ukrainian Soldiers' Mothers Ask Sons to Keep Away from Crackdown." *International Business Times*, 23 January 2014. Accessed 5 March 2015. http://www.ibtimes.co.uk/kiev-protests-ukrainian-soldiers-mothers-ask-sons-keep-away-crackdown-1433432.

Stebelsky, Ihor. "The Resettlement of Ukrainian Refugees in Canada after the Second World War." In *Canada's Ukrainians: Negotiating an Identity*, edited by Lubomyr Luciuk and Stella Hryniuk. 1–35. Toronto: University of Toronto Press, 1991.

Subtelny, Orest. *Ukraine: A History*, 3rd ed. Toronto: University of Toronto Press, 2000.

Suchaka, Weronika. "'*Za Hranetsiu*' – 'Beyond the Border': Constructions of Identities in Ukrainian-Canadian Literature." PhD diss., Greifswald University, 2011.

Suknaski, Andrew. *The Name of Narid*. Erin Mills: Porcupine's Quill, 1981.

– *Wood Mountain Poems*. Toronto: Macmillan, 1976.

Swyripa, Frances. *Wedded to the Cause: Ukrainian Canadian Women and Ethnic Identity, 1891–1991*. Toronto: University of Toronto Press, 1993.

Wah, Fred. *Faking It: Poetics and Hybridity, Critical Writing 1984–1999*. Edmonton: NeWest Press, 2000.

Wawryshyn, Olena. Interview with Lisa Grekul. Новий шлях / *The New Pathway* 19 (2006): 8.

Wexler, Laura. "Saying Good-Bye to 'Once Upon a Time,' or Implementing Postmodernism in Creative Nonfiction." In *Writing Creative Non-Fiction*, edited by Carolyn Forche and Philip Gerard. 25–33. Cincinnati: Story Press, 2001.

Williamson, Judith. "Seeing Spots." *City Limits*, 25 March 1983.

Woycenko, Ol'ha. *The Ukrainians in Canada*. Winnipeg: Trident Press, 1968.

Contributors

Elizabeth Bachinsky is the author of three collections of poetry: *Curio* (2005), *Home of Sudden Service* (2006), and *God of Missed Connections* (2009). Her work has been nominated for the Pat Lowther Award (2010), the Kobzar Literary Award (2010), the George Ryga Award for Social Awareness in Literature (2010), the Governor General's Award for Poetry (2006), and the Bronwen Wallace Award (2004) and has appeared in literary journals, anthologies, and on film in Canada, the United States, France, Ireland, England, China, and Lebanon. She lives in East Vancouver, where she is an instructor in creative writing and an editor for *Event* magazine.

Marusya Bociurkiw is a writer, media artist, and teacher. She has a PhD in Interdisciplinary Studies and is the author of the short story collection *The Woman Who Loved Airports* (1994), a collection of poetry, *Halfway to the East* (1999), a novel, *The Children of Mary* (2006), and her widely celebrated and award-winning memoir, *Comfort Food for Breakups* (2007). The latter was a finalist for the Golden Crown Literary Award, Lesbian Short Story Essay Collection Winner, Independent Publisher Award (SILVER), Autobiography/Memoir Winner, ForeWord Magazine Book of the Year Award (GOLD), and was short-listed for the Lambda literary award and the Kobzar Literary Award. Her stories, essays, and articles have been widely anthologized in collections and journals. She has written and directed nine films and videos that have been screened worldwide.

Lisa Grekul completed her BA and MA degrees at the University of Alberta. She holds a PhD from the University of British Columbia. Lisa is a creative writer and literary scholar whose research focuses on Canadian literature (minority/diasporic writers, in particular), other postcolonial literatures, and postcolonial theory. Her first novel, *Kalyna's Song* (2003), is a coming-of-age story about a third-generation Ukrainian Canadian girl who grows up in northeastern Alberta and southern Africa. Her second book, *Leaving Shadows: Literature in English by Canada's Ukrainians* (2005), is a critical study of English-language Ukrainian Canadian poetry, drama, fiction, and creative non-fiction. Currently she is an Associate Professor of English in the Faculty of Creative and Critical Studies at the University of British Columbia Okanagan.

Myrna Kostash is a full-time non-fiction writer and author of ten books, including the classic *All of Baba's Children* (1977) and its follow-up *All of Baba's Great Grandchildren* (2000). Her travel memoir *Bloodlines: A Journey into Eastern Europe* (1993) was touted as one of the "ten best books of the year!" by *Maclean's* magazine. Besides writing for diverse magazines (from *Border Crossings* to *Maclean's*), Kostash has written for theatre cabaret, radio documentary, and television documentary. As one of Canada's best-known writer-exponents of creative non-fiction, she has been writer-in-residence in Minneapolis, Minnesota, and at the University of Alberta, and Ashley Fellow at Trent University. She has lectured throughout Canada and eastern and southeastern Europe. Her most recent work, *Prodigal Daughter: A Journey to Byzantium*, was published in 2010, when she was also awarded the Matt Cohen Award for lifetime achievement in writing. Forthcoming in 2016 is *Battle of Seven Oaks: A Reader*.

Janice Kulyk Keefer received her BA from the University of Toronto and her MPhil and DPhil from the University of Sussex. She is the author of over a dozen works of poetry, prose, and literary criticism. Among her awards are first prize in the CBC radio literary competition and the National Magazine Award, the 13th Marian Engel Award, and a SSHRCC artist/researcher fellowship. *Under Eastern Eyes* (1987), her study of Canadian fiction from the Maritimes, and her novel *The Green Library* (1996), were both shortlisted for a Governor General's award. *Marrying the Sea* (1998), a collection of poetry, won the Canadian Authors' Award, and her most recent novel, *The Ladies Lending Library* (2007), won the Kobzar prize. Among her publications are a family memoir, *Honey and Ashes* (1998), *Foreign Relations* (2010), a volume of poetry produced in collaboration with painter Natalka Husar, and a pendant to the latter's book of paintings, *Burden of Innocence*. She is a Professor Emeritus of English at the University of Guelph and also teaches in Guelph-Humber's MFA in Creative Writing Program.

Lindy Ledohowski completed her BA (Hons.) at the University of Manitoba and her BEd, MA, and PhD at the University of Toronto, and completed a postdoctoral fellowship at the University of Ottawa. She was an Assistant Professor in the Department of English at St Jerome's University in the University of Waterloo before becoming an Adjunct Research Professor at Carleton University. She is a scholar of contemporary Canadian identity politics and has published numerous scholarly articles on this topic – often through an English-language, Ukrainian Canadian literary case study. She is also an award-winning educational expert and a member of the Board of Trustees for the Canadian Museum for Human Rights.

Erín Moure, a Montreal poet, has published seventeen books of poetry as well as a volume of essays, *My Beloved Wager*. She is also a translator from French, Spanish, Galician (galego), and Portuguese, with eleven books translated, of work by poets as diverse as Nicole Brossard, Andrés Ajens, Louise Dupré, and Fernando Pessoa. Her work has received the Governor General's Award, the Pat Lowther Memorial Award, and the A.M. Klein Prize (twice), and she had been a three-time finalist for the Griffin Poetry Prize. Moure holds an honorary doctorate from Brandon University. Her latest works are the Kobzar literary prize short-listed collection *The Unmemntioable*, an investigation into subjectivity and wartime experience in western Ukraine and the South Peace region of Alberta; *Kapusta*; and *Insecession*, published in a single volume with her translation of Chus Pato's *Secession*.

Daria Salamon holds BAs in Arts and in Education from the Universities of Winnipeg and Manitoba. She teaches creative writing at Red River College. As a writer, she has contributed to the *Globe and Mail* and *Prairie Fire Magazine* and has been a columnist for the *Winnipeg Free Press*. Her short fiction and creative non-fiction have been shortlisted for the Writers' Union of Canada's Emerging Writer Short Fiction Award. She published her best-selling first novel *The Prairie Bridesmaid* in 2008. It won the Eileen McTavish Sykes Award for Best First Book; it was shortlisted for several other writing awards, and Foreword Magazine identified it as an Honourable Mention in the Best General Fiction category. *The Prairie Bridesmaid* has been optioned for film, and Salamon recently adapted the novel into a screenplay. She has just finished writing her second novel, *Push*.

Marsha Forchuk Skrypuch has received a long list of awards for her nineteen books, the most recent being back-to-back Silver Birch Award wins: in 2013 for *Making Bombs for Hitler* and in 2014 for *One Step at a Time: A Vietnamese Child Finds Her Way*. She also received the 2014 Manitoba Young Readers' Choice Award for *Making Bombs for Hitler* and the B.C. Red Cedar Information Book Award for *Last Airlift: A Vietnamese Orphan's Rescue from War*. Her most cherished award is the Order of Princess Olha, bestowed upon her personally in 2008 by President Yuschenko in recognition of *Enough*, the first commercially available book to be set during the Holodomor. Marsha had received death threats and hate mail for writing on this topic. Marsha has an Honours BA in English Literature and a Master of Library Science degree, both from the University of Western Ontario.

Weronika Suchacka comes from Poland. She holds a BA from the University of Szczecin, Poland, as well as an MA and a PhD from the University of Greifswald, Germany. She was granted the Mecklenburg–Western Pomerania State Scholarship to do her Master's studies, and later she received the State Scholarship for Doctoral Students to pursue her PhD, which she received in 2011, having defended her thesis "'Za Hranetsiu' – 'Beyond the Border': Constructions of Identities in Ukrainian-Canadian Literature." She is now employed at the University of Szczecin, where, among other subjects, she teaches Ukrainian Canadian literature, and where, in 2011, she co-founded (together with Hartmut Lutz and Uwe Zagratzki) the Szczecin Canadian Studies Group (SCSG).